OVERVIEW

Overview

Can you say for sure whether your team or employee goals are consistently being met? It's important to know if everyone is working to the standards expected of them. Effective performance management can help boost productivity at all levels of your organization.

A systematic approach is important to increase productivity throughout an organization. It's also important to focus on achieving results that contribute to the success of a company. These are two cornerstones of effective performance management.

This course begins with an explanation of the nature of performance management and the advantages it provides to organizations that use it. Then the five phases that typically comprise a performance management system will be introduced. Much of the course is an in-depth look at the first phase, planning for performance, and it also covers how to establish performance expectations.

During this first phase of the performance management process, you'll establish critical success factors and translate them into key performance indicators. Then you'll develop role profiles to help match people with the right skills to appropriate work – further improving performance.

Once you've completed this course, you'll have an understanding of what a performance management system involves and be able to undertake the planning needed for such a system to be effective. This planning is the basis for all the other phases of performance management.

Monitoring performance is critically important. It shows you whether you're on track to achieve your goals. And, if you're not, it gives you the chance to change things before it's too late.

You can only monitor and measure performance when you have clear and specific targets and standards. You also need to be able to collect the right performance data – and know how to analyze it, use it, and act on it. Finally, you must know how to deal effectively with underperformance, whether that's from employees who aren't performing, can't perform, or won't perform to the standard required.

This course introduces a four-step process for monitoring and improving performance. It first explains how to determine and set appropriate targets and standards against which you can measure performance. It then introduces different ways to collect the relevant data, and shows you how to analyze the data and decide on appropriate action to help respond to gaps in performance. Finally, the course presents a technique for dealing with under-performers in a positive and collaborative way.

Performance Management

Managing the performance of your employees is an essential part of being a manager. And one of the most important parts of managing performance is taking a strategic, integrated, and cohesive approach to rewarding employees for the value they produce for the organization.

Reward management is a process of formulating and implementing policies, strategies, and practices to reward employees fairly, consistently, and in line with their value to the organization. It's important that employees understand that there's a clear connection between how well they perform and how well they're rewarded. An effective reward system organizes and categorizes reward-related processes and activities to ensure that reward management produces value for both employees and employer.

Performance appraisal is the part of reward management that involves monitoring, measuring, and assessing how well employees meet the standards and competency requirements of their jobs. Put simply, performance appraisal puts a value on an employee's contribution to the organization.

The assessment of an employee's performance is communicated to the employee through the performance appraisal meeting. This is a formal discussion about how well that person has achieved the key outcomes or goals of the job over a period of time. But an appraisal meeting needs to be handled well if it's going to result in a positive and productive experience for both manager and employee.

This course covers reviewing and rewarding performance. You'll discover how to apply a system to rate employee performance. You'll determine the right approach to conduct performance appraisal meetings. You'll also learn to recognize the benefits of both extrinsic and intrinsic rewards practices, as well as how to determine performance-based pay percentages.

CHAPTER 1 - Planning for Performance
CHAPTER 1 - Planning for Performance
  Section 1 - Benefits of Performance Management
  Section 2 - Using a Performance Management System
  Section 3 - Establishing Expectations
  Section 4 - Developing Role Profiles

Section 1 - Benefits of Performance Management

Section 1 - Benefits of Performance Management

Performance is about results that contribute to the success of an organization. It depends on collective effort. To achieve the most, the three levels of performance – organization, process, and individual – need to be aligned.

There are five key benefits to maintaining a performance management system. It focuses attention on results, aligns organizational activities and processes with organizational goals, nurtures a holistic and long-term view of the organization, produces meaningful measurements, and improves morale and productivity.

Understanding performance management

Understanding performance management

For an organization to be successful, performance needs to occur on three levels. The organization supporting the work, the processes guiding the work, and the individuals contributing to the work all need to be working together toward successful outcomes. If a breakdown occurs at any of these levels, it will diminish performance. When this is the case, you'll need to take action to improve what's not working so optimal performance can be achieved.

Organization

The organization level is the foundation for the other two levels of performance. It includes the culture, mission, strategy, and policies that support and allow work to be done. These must all be aligned with one another for the organization to thrive.

For example, a company, whose mission is to be on the cutting-edge of technology, doesn't support team building exercises. As such, teams are less likely to collaborate and generate creative ideas.

Processes

All work is done at the process level. Workflow, job design, and required inputs and outputs must be designed and organized to meet organizational goals.

For example, two sales teams for a national communications company aren't meeting telephone sales quotas because the process doesn't specify the number of calls required to reach the expected output.

Individuals

Individual employees affect the processes. Contributing factors at the individual level include individual performance goals, knowledge, skills, work environment, availability of support tools, coaching, and feedback. If performance isn't optimal, investigate whether employees are actually being supported in their work.

For example, a new employee working in a claims processing branch of a major insurance company processes 30% fewer claims per week than the average employee because her manager is not providing the necessary training.

Aims of performance management systems

You may have noted that all performance management systems share some common aims. One overarching aim is to increase the overall effectiveness of the organization. Building on the desire to increase effectiveness, organizations typically work to establish a high-performance culture where individuals and teams take responsibility for continuous improvement.

Performance Management

And because employees contribute so much to the overall performance of an organization, optimizing individual performance is a key goal. Performance management systems are built to help people focus on doing what's necessary to be successful. And in support of individuals, performance management systems are designed to empower, motivate, and reward employees to do their best, and to align their individual objectives with corporate plans.

Three factors are needed to make performance management successful. First, the organization must communicate clear expectations. The reason is simple – employees tend to meet or exceed expectations when they know exactly what's expected of them.

Second, the organization must involve employees in the process. Managers and employees must work in partnership to develop expectations that work for them both. For instance, how committed would you be to expectations that, when achieved, would mean your work conditions or career would be negatively impacted? While compromise may be necessary, both parties need to feel like they'll benefit from the achievement of the mutually agreed upon expectations.

And finally, the organization must use a systematic approach. Effective performance management systems comprise a series of related activities and while they're performed individually, together they contribute to the success of the whole. So, the better each activity is performed, the better an organization's overall performance.

Question

Which statements describe the key aspects of performance management?

Options:

1. Expectations must be communicated to make performance management work
2. Employees are involved in the process of performance management
3. Performance management is a systematic but flexible process
4. Performance expectations are provided to employees to guide their work
5. Performance is measured in terms of quality in a performance management system

Answer

Option 1: This option is correct. The focus provided by clear expectations helps employees and teams be more productive because they understand what they need to do.

Option 2: This option is correct. Performance management is a partnership between management and employees, where both feel they'll benefit from the expectations they set.

Option 3: This option is correct. Using a systematic approach to performance management helps make sure all activities work together to contribute to the overall success of the organization.

Option 4: This option is incorrect. Performance expectations need to be developed in partnership with employees, not simply provided to them.

Option 5: This option is incorrect. Performance is the collective effort that generates a result or output.

The value of performance management

The value of performance management

Why develop and maintain a performance management system? Using a performance management system does take work, but it's worth the effort. There are five ways in which such a system will tend to increase productivity and organizational success. It concentrates on results, aligns organizational activities with goals, nurtures a holistic and long-term view of the organization, produces meaningful measurements, and improves morale.

Why is concentrating on results an advantage? Typically, it's more supportive of improved effectiveness. As such, organizations that implement performance management systems are more open to change that increases productivity.

For example, suppose an automaker has a traditional, rigid design process. But the company feels this rigid process is stifling creativity. It introduces a more flexible process for finding innovative, viable solutions more quickly. Because it is focused on results – the quality and speed of design – it is open to change that improves organizational effectiveness.

One related advantage of concentrating on results is that it builds objective support when an employee needs to be let go for inadequate performance. Also, it tends to raise performance expectations and to improve the quality and timeliness of information.

The second advantage of performance management is that it aligns organizational activities and processes with goals, helping to optimize operations. By identifying goals, results needed to achieve those goals, and measures of effectiveness in moving toward those goals, performance management tends to optimize operations. In the example of the automaker, engineers set an objective to improve braking system reliability by 20% over two years. This aligns with the company's mission of providing the safest vehicles.

You may have noted that there's a clear connection between what you, or your department does and what your organization hopes to achieve. If so, this perspective will likely help you to focus on continuously improving performance.

The third advantage of performance management is that it nurtures a holistic and long-term view of the organization. This enables organizations to achieve a better understanding of what's best for the entire company.

Returning to the example of the automaker, senior management is looking for ways to continuously improve performance. Realizing that its employees are a great resource, it establishes a program to encourage employees to share their ideas about how to improve performance. The program includes rewards for contributing.

In adopting a holistic and long-term view, the automaker is able to achieve continuous improvement. The fourth advantage of performance management is that it allows organizations to produce meaningful measurements. These measurements can be used for benchmarking within the organization or to compare best practices with those of other successful organizations.

Measurements can also be used to indicate the results of improvement initiatives such as training, management development, and quality programs.

The automaker establishes a benchmark on a key performance metric – smart technology. It will use these measures to compare itself with other automakers in its class. Based on what's revealed, the company can target its performance improvement efforts to be more competitive in this area.

The fifth advantage of performance management is that it can improve morale and productivity. Because individuals will understand what they should be doing and why, what's expected of them, and how their work contributes to the goals of the organization, they'll work more independently and make better decisions every day. All this will improve performance.

For example, the automaker's finance officer knows she's expected to offer customers better financing options when possible. She knows this increases customer value and satisfaction, helps the company reach its sales goals, and helps advance her career.

Because she understands the implications of her actions and that they impact the organization's overall success, she pursues all opportunities to offer better financing to customers.

Question

Which statements properly express the value organizations derive from a performance management system?

Options:

1. Performance management focuses on results as a means to direct and evaluate performance
2. Activities and processes are aligned with the performance expectations of leaders in the same field
3. Decisions are made and expectations are set based on what is best for the entire organization over the long-term
4. Measurements are generated to help make sure improvement initiatives are effective
5. Personal morale and productivity increase due to increased direction from managers on day-to-day tasks

Answer

Option 1: This option is correct. By focusing on results the efforts of individuals and teams are directly related to organizational success.

Option 2: This option is incorrect. Activities and processes are aligned with organizational goals. This helps ensure that all efforts are targeted to accomplishing the same goals, which is ultimately most productive.

Option 3: This option is correct. Instead of taking fragmented action, all efforts are coordinated to improve organizational success. This in turn tends to improve the performance of teams and individuals alike.

Performance Management

Option 4: This option is correct. An organization using a performance management system uses measurements to determine the effectiveness of its improvement initiatives.

Option 5: This option is incorrect. Because employees know what's expected of them and how they contribute to success, they'll be capable of making more meaningful contributions, without being micromanaged.

Section 2 - Using a Performance Management System

Section 2 - Using a Performance Management System

Using the five-phase performance management process can help your organization continuously improve performance in the pursuit of optimal performance. The planning phase is when expectations are established. During the monitoring phase data is collected to make sure performance is on track to achieving expectations. The third phase involves taking steps to improve performance. The review phase identifies employee weaknesses and strengths to better target improvements. The fifth phase is about rewarding employees appropriately as an incentive to continue delivering high performance.

Plan

Plan

An effective performance management system has five phases – plan, monitor, improve, review, and reward performance. Implementing each phase correctly helps ensure a smooth process, because each phase depends on the effectiveness of the phase before it.

In the planning phase, you establish performance expectations. This involves working with your team members to determine expectations, to align indicators of performance with overall corporate strategy, and to create role profiles that support expectations.

Determine expectations

You must determine expectations by mutual consent with the people involved. The better defined expectations are, the more likely they are to be achieved.

For example, a copy editor and his manager agree that he'll use a new editorial process to eliminate copy errors.

Align indicators with strategy

Once you've determined the expectations, you need to align the relevant performance indicators with overall corporate strategy. This helps ensure that individual goals help to achieve the overall corporate strategy.

Carrying on with the example of the copy editor, eliminating copy errors aligns with the corporate strategy of improving the overall quality of the company's publications.

Create role profiles

The final activity when planning for performance is to create role profiles. Role profiles outline what the employee must do to meet the performance expectations of the role. Once role profiles are created, performance plans are developed as a way to objectively measure performance.

Again the copy editor and his manager work together to create a profile that emphasizes that the key responsibility of the role is to eliminate copy errors. It also provides guidance on what tools, resources, and processes are available to accomplish expectations of the role.

Monitor

Monitor

The second phase of performance management is monitoring performance. Tracking performance lets you know if current performance will deliver on expectations. Of course, you can monitor performance only if you've already clearly set the performance expectations. During the monitoring phase asking questions can help you track and evaluate performance. For instance, "Are we on track?" and "What gaps in performance exist?"

You can use monitoring tools to collect data and observe performance.

However, managers and employees need to agree on the data collection method.

They also need to agree on what's being monitored and how the results will be interpreted.

Once you know what you're monitoring, you can use tools to help you monitor performance. Charts are a basic but very effective tool to track performance. A manager may use a chart outlining agreed performance metrics to measure an employee's progress. For instance, the chart might track progress toward improving accuracy in completing customer requests for service.

Dashboards are an engaging visual tool for analyzing key metrics. An accountant might use a dashboard to help track depreciation and amortization of the company's capital assets, for example.

Six Sigma is a management philosophy that emphasizes setting objectives, collecting data, and analyzing results to reduce defects in products and services. An auto manufacturer may use Six Sigma to identify inefficiencies in the painting process. Once identified, the company takes action to improve the efficiency of the process, thereby improving performance.

When monitoring performance, you need to identify performance gaps. A gap is the difference between desired and actual performance. Once you know what the performance gaps are, you can then take steps to improve performance.

For example, a manager in an accounting firm identifies a performance gap. Several accountants need to upgrade their auditing skills in order to be more proficient. Their manager arranges for these employees to attend training to upgrade their professional accreditation.

Question

Match each example to the related phase of the performance management process. Each step may have more than one match.

Options:

Performance Management

A. A manager and his team outline what needs to be done to meet the expectation of improved output and how it'll be achieved

B. A supervisor uses Six Sigma to determine if machinists creating custom parts can work efficiently with available resources

C. A sales manager uses an operational dashboard to help her representatives reach their daily sales quotas

D. A team and its leader determine that following all safety procedures is imperative to achieving performance expectations

Targets:
1. Plan
2. Monitor

Answer

Determining expectations, including what and how they'll be achieved, are part of planning for performance.

Tools such as Six Sigma and dashboards can be used to monitor performance. What's learned can help identify performance gaps.

Improve

Improve
Phase three of the performance management process is to improve performance. The goal of this phase is to ensure that employees constantly develop. It's at this phase that you'll address the performance gaps identified in phase two.

The first thing you need to do is perform a gap analysis. A gap analysis is used to determine the difference between desired and actual performance. As you do, make sure you clearly understand why performance isn't meeting expectations.

A performance gap is usually caused by a lack of resources or other necessary factors such as knowledge, skills, feedback and motivation.

Performance gaps can also be caused by task interference. For example, a worker's efforts may be inhibited by a micromanaging supervisor or by a manager who sets conflicting deadlines. Such actions may undermine the quality of the employee's work.

Now that you understand the gaps, you can use techniques to improve performance. Techniques include training, providing targeted feedback, creating development plans, which might involve assigning new responsibilities, and coaching or mentoring.

A variety of tools can be used to deliver these techniques. For example, depending on your needs, you may choose to deliver training via online courses, by delivering seminars, or providing resource books, for example.

John, an insurance company team manager, is worried about the number of policies being sold. A preliminary investigation uncovers a performance gap. The expectation is that 30% of leads will result in policy sales, but presently only 17% of leads are translating into sales.

After performing a gap analysis, John finds that many agents lack the skills to close sales successfully.

John decides to tackle the issue head on. He designs a training program and arranges for all agents to attend the skills building workshop.

Question

Which statements about performance gaps are accurate?

Options:

1. A gap analysis is used to identify performance gaps

2. A performance gap is the difference between desired and actual performance

3. Performance gaps are always related to poor work practices

4. A common use of gap analysis is to focus on improving corporate image

Answer

Option 1: This option is correct. The purpose of a gap analysis is to identify areas where performance isn't achieving what's expected.

Option 2: This option is correct. A performance gap is defined as the difference between desired, or expected, performance and the level of performance actually being achieved.

Option 3: This option is incorrect. Sometimes performance gaps are the result of poor work practices, however, communication problems and task interference are also common causes of performance gaps.

Option 4: This option is incorrect. Performance management systems use gap analysis to aid in performance improvement efforts – not to improve the company's image.

Review

Review

The fourth phase, reviewing performance, aims to keep performance on track. You can help keep performance on track by providing positive or corrective feedback and completing performance reviews. Rating and upgrading development plans and identifying employee strengths and weaknesses can also be effective ways to keep performance on track.

You may find it useful to use certain tools to review performance to determine if it's on track. These tools include rating records and formal performance appraisals.

A rating record is a tool used to evaluate employee performance against standards set for the tasks that make up a role. They summarize employee performance during a particular appraisal period and may be part of the organization's performance review process. Performance appraisals are used to assess employee performance. The goal of performance appraisals is to encourage continued areas of desired performance and address areas where improvement is required.

For instance, the manager of a software development team conducts annual performance appraisals. One employee's appraisal shows that the employee could improve her programming skills. But the manager might also see that this employee excels in situations where she's in a leadership role.

Question

Match each example to the phase of the performance management process where it belongs. Each phase may apply to more than one example.

Options:

A. A supervisor recognizes an employee's improved performance and gives him positive encouragement

B. A performance gap indicates that training is needed for employees to meet expectations

C. A manager notices that an employee is having a hard time expressing her ideas and targets this for improvement

D. A manager develops a mentoring program to help employees improve their leadership skills

Targets:

1. Improve
2. Review

Answer

Improving performance is a continuous process and may include activities like training and mentoring. Positive encouragement and planning ways to overcome weaknesses are part of the review step.

Reward

Reward

The fifth and final phase of the performance management process is to reward employees. The goal is to encourage optimal performance. Rewarding employees is key to having happy and productive employees. This can help to maintain the productivity of high-performing employees and motivate less productive employees to strive to achieve higher performance. Additionally, rewards help attract driven employees.

A good strategy is to align performance with rewards. This way, employees know what they're working toward, which provides the motivation to perform well. Recognizing employees for good work and the use of bonus and incentive plans are examples of how to link performance with rewards.

For example, a publicly traded company offers its employees the option to invest in the company.

Employees appreciate the opportunity to purchase shares at a lower rate. And because employees make money when the company does well, it provides another incentive for them to contribute to and achieve optimal performance.

Pay scales – wage ranges for particular work – can also provide incentive. For instance, if performance is directly related to pay, employees may perform better to get a pay raise.

Agreed-on rewards between employee and management can also be useful incentives for improved and sustained performance. This strategy allows rewards to be targeted to individual employees.

For instance, an employee may prefer more vacation time over benefits. Another employee may value company stock options more than a higher salary.

Question

Match each example to the relevant phase of the performance management process.

Options:

A. Tanya agrees that she's expected to hit milestones 98% of the time

B. Observation and interpretation of production outputs indicate a performance gap exists

C. A team manager uses training to address the team's inability to close sales

D. Janet's performance review shows she'd perform better if she had better communication skills

E. Based on Tom's performance review, his manager recommends Tom receive a pay raise

Targets:

1. Plan

Performance Management

2. Monitor
3. Improve
4. Review
5. Reward

Answer

In the planning phase, expectations are defined to establish what's necessary to meet organizational objectives.

After interpreting performance data, it may be clear that performance gaps are limiting performance.

The improvement phase involves efforts to either boost performance by addressing performance gaps or facilitating efficiencies, for example.

During the review phase, areas in need of improvement are identified. This process can feed into improvement efforts. The review phase is also an opportunity to notice employee strengths and to give encouragement.

Rewards are an effective way to recognize the efforts of employees who perform well and to encourage them to continuously improve their performance.

Section 3 - Establishing Expectations
Section 3 - Establishing Expectations

Planning is the first step in the process for managing performance. It's here that you determine what's necessary to be successful – performance expectations.

Critical success factors provide direction on what's important. These are the actions or areas where success is necessary for the organization to achieve its strategic objectives, goals, and mission.

Key performance indicators are specific measures used to quantify CSFs. They allow performance toward achieving CSFs to be assessed. Create effective KPIs by making sure each one is relevant, quantifiable, clear, and focused.

Understanding CSFs

Understanding CSFs

Planning for performance management requires you to perform three actions – identify critical success factors, establish key performance indicators, and develop role profiles for performance agreement. While each element is vital to planning, they're not sequential. The order presented here is typical, but the elements should be applied in a way that best suits your circumstances.

Effectively planning for performance means providing direction on what's important – that is, what needs to be accomplished for successful outcomes.

Ultimately, success is accomplishing the strategic objectives designed to make sure the company achieves its mission. This requires you to determine which actions or areas are crucial to achieving objectives.

The areas or actions identified as necessary to achieving objectives are known as critical success factors, or CSFs.

Generally, CSFs are key areas where things must go right or key activities that must be done right for the business, unit, or team to be successful.

For example, suppose an organization's mission statement is to provide reliable products. In support of its mission the organization sets a strategic goal to grow revenue by 20% this quarter.

In line with this mission and strategic goal, the organization develops strategic objectives to help grow revenue. One such objective may be to increase consumer trust in the product.

After exploring what will have to be done to achieve this objective, the development team identifies CSFs. Attracting new customers and selling more to existing customers are both set as CSFs.

Establishing CSFs

Because CSFs represent areas or activities that are imperative to organizational success, they're an important component of your performance management efforts. Given their role, you need to be sure to establish the right CSFs for your unit.

Perhaps you found it difficult to pinpoint the areas or activities that need to be addressed to achieve your team's goals. But there's a three-step method to help you do just that. First, establish the unit's mission and strategic objectives, then generate potential CSFs, and finally select the ones that best fit.

You begin by clarifying your unit's mission and strategic objectives or goals. Because these are what defines success, they should guide all the organization's activities toward achieving its goals.

Your CSFs need to align directly with the mission statement and strategic goals up to the highest level.

For example, consider the mission statement of an electronics company. Its mission is to become the largest supplier of personal light therapy devices in the industry by growing its sales in this category by 15%.

Based on this mission, one strategic objective may be to increase market share by 10% in the coming fiscal year. Another may be to increase web-based marketing by 50%. Both are directly related to achieving the company's mission.

In step two of identifying CSFs, you brainstorm potential CSFs for each strategic objective identified in step one. It's helpful to consider the four types of CSFs – industry specific, environmental, strategic, and organizational. This makes it more likely you'll be able to come up with a full range of possible CSFs.

Industry specific

Industry-specific factors arise as a result of the nature of the industry and concern activities an organization must do to remain competitive.

Suppose an automobile manufacturer is competing against other manufacturers who emphasize fuel economy. Recognizing this, it sets an objective to improve fuel economy by 12%. A related CSF may be to increase research and development efforts to develop a more aerodynamic car.

Environmental

Environmental factors are the influences outside a company that impact it. These factors include business climate, the economy, competitors, and technological advancements.

For instance, a retailer with an objective related to increasing its market share may identify a CSF to increase its web presence to reach new customers.

Strategic

Strategic factors stem from the competitive strategy being pursued by the organization. These factors are related to how the company positions and markets itself.

For instance, does the company want to be high-volume, low-cost or low-volume, high-cost? If one of its strategic objectives is to provide low-volume, high-cost products, a CSF may be to achieve superior quality by using the best materials.

Organizational

Organizational factors stem from internal forces. The challenges, opportunities, and influences an organization faces, as well as the direction it chooses, will determine these factors.

For instance, if an organization chooses to produce a high volume of low-cost products, its manufacturing process will focus on speed, not quality. A resulting CSF may be to improve the efficiency of the manufacturing process.

Finally, in step three, you need to evaluate the possible CSFs. The aim is to identify which of the possible CSFs are essential to successfully achieve the strategic objectives they relate to.

For example, a major book retailer has set a strategic objective to open two new stores to attract new customers. Potential CSFs may be to secure financing for the expansion, to manage the builds to avoid delays and mistakes, and to increase advertising in the two areas where the stores will open.

Securing the financing for the expansion is a CSF because without the financing, the expansion isn't possible. And while managing the builds and increasing advertising are important, the managers are likely to decide that they aren't as important to achieving the strategic objective as making sure the financing is available.

Consider this example of a consulting firm identifying CSFs based on its mission and strategic objective.

Its mission is to be the number one social media consulting firm to the insurance industry by providing relevant advice to clients and having 96% customer satisfaction.

Building from its mission, the team establishes the strategic objectives involved in achieving its mission. Strategic objectives that align with its mission include: "increasing market share by 20%," "being the leader in our field to ensure we provide relevant advice," and "sustaining a customer satisfaction rate of 96%."

Now the team needs to identify potential CSFs relevant to those objectives. Through brainstorming, the team generates five possible CSFs: attract and satisfy new customers, increase competitiveness versus other social media consulting firms, remain knowledgeable through leadership in the field, provide excellent customer service, and retain staff and continue with customer-centric training.

Question

Match the potential CSFs to the type of CSF it is. Each type may apply to more than one CSF.

Options:

A. Attract and satisfy new customers

B. Increase competitiveness versus other social media consulting firms

C. Remain knowledgeable through leadership in the field

D. Provide excellent customer service

E. Retain staff and continue with customer-centric training

Targets:
1. Strategic
2. Environmental
3. Industry specific
4. Organizational

Answer

Attracting and satisfying new customers and remaining knowledgeable through leadership in the field are strategic CSFs. Both are related to choices the company has made about how to conduct business.

Increasing competitiveness versus other social media consulting firms is an environmental CSF. This CSF relates to an outside influence – competition.

Providing excellent customer service is an industry-specific CSF. This stems from the nature of the industry and the company must be successful to remain competitive.

Retaining staff and continuing with customer-centric training is an organizational CSF. This is an internal goal that the company needs to achieve.

Finally based on the potential CSFs, the team decides which are the most critical. First, it decides that attracting and satisfying new customers is essential. Otherwise the team can't achieve the objective of being the number one provider of social media advice. Second, remaining knowledgeable through leadership in the field is identified as a CSF. And third, the team must retain staff and continue with customer-centric training if it's to sustain a 96% customer satisfaction rate.

Question

A sporting goods manufacturer's mission is to be the number one choice of professionals by delivering top quality and leading-edge sports equipment while achieving a 95% satisfaction rating.

Match each strategic goal with the example CSF that corresponds to it.

Options:

A. Grow business in a tough economic climate

B. Create constant demand among professional customers

C. Provide the highest quality equipment

D. Improve manufacturing methods

Targets:

1. Beat competitors to the market with revolutionary products

2. Sustain demand during economic downturns

3. Create high-quality sports equipment targeted to professionals

4. Overcome barriers to using new materials

Answer

To remain competitive the manufacturer must beat its competitors to the market. This is an example of an industry-specific CSF.

Sustaining demand for its products during an economic downturn is an example of an environmental CSF. Environmental CSFs are external to the company and outside its control.

Choosing to create high quality sports equipment targeted to professionals is a specific competitive strategy and is an example of a strategic CSF.

Overcoming barriers is an internal factor and is therefore an example of an organizational CSF.

Establishing KPIs

Establishing KPIs

Once CSFs have been identified, you need to determine how to measure whether they're being achieved. The second action for planning for performance is establishing key performance indicators, or KPIs. KPIs quantify CSFs and therefore provide a way to measure progress toward achieving them. Without the ability to measure CSFs, you can't determine whether strategic objectives are being, or will be, met.

Given a CSF to increase sales in international markets, an appropriate KPI might be to measure the percentage of income the company derives from international sales in a quarter.

Or given the CSF to provide efficient service, an insurance company may create several KPIs to measure this. For example, a KPI may be to reply to customers with nonemergency claims within 12 hours. Other possible KPIs might be to process 95% of claims within 48 hours of receipt, and to identify the percentage of claims paid within 30 days of receipt.

These KPIs enable the organization to use the data collected to measure performance and progress made toward achieving its CSFs, objectives, and goals.

Typically, different types of KPIs are needed to fully understand your unit's performance. These KPIs include process, input, and output KPIs.

Process

Process KPIs measure efficiency or productivity of business processes. For instance, turnaround time for orders, time-to-market of new products, or time to answer customer inquires may be relevant KPIs.

Input

Input KPIs measure assets and resources invested to generate business results. Input KPIs include money spent on research and development and raw materials, and hours spent by employees producing goods or services.

Output

Output KPIs measure financial and non-financial results of business activities, quantity, or quality. Customer satisfaction, revenues, and the number of services provided are examples of output KPIs.

Effective KPIs contain a number of important elements:
- they specify the purpose of KPI, and the reason the measure is needed,
- they specify the relevant strategic objective,
- they develop the targets that will allow you to evaluate performance,

- they provide a formula for how performance will be measured,
- they identify who will take the measurements and how often, and
- they establish who will act on the data and how.

Question

Which statements accurately describe what you need to do when creating a KPI?

Options:

1. Explain why the KPI is being created
2. Name the strategic objective it is intended to quantify
3. Provide relevant targets established to measure success
4. Outline alternative measurement methods to pick from as the work progresses
5. Identify who'll take performance measurements
6. Allow for discretion when the time comes to decide who will act on the data and how

Answer

Option 1: This option is correct. You need to define the purpose of the KPI.

Option 2: This option is correct. KPIs are designed to quantify CSFs that are directly related to strategic objectives. An effective KPI names the objective it relates to.

Option 3: This option is correct. Targets are used to evaluate performance.

Option 4: This option is incorrect. The method for measuring results must be selected as the KPI is created.

Option 5: This option is correct. Part of creating the KPI is to state who will take measurements.

Option 6: This option is incorrect. When developing KPIs, it's important to identify not only who will use the data, but also how it will be used.

When creating KPIs, ensure they're relevant, quantifiable, clear, and focused.

Relevant

KPIs align with the success of the organization, so to be relevant they must support organizational goals. Specifically, they support strategic objectives, which in turn align with organizational goals. So, for instance, if the goal is to improve sales, the KPI must support this by being designed to measure sales.

Quantifiable

Effective KPIs are quantifiable. Create KPIs that provide ways to monitor and measure performance and that will help achieve them. What you can measure, you can achieve. Be sure to include meaningful thresholds, targets, and benchmarks.

Clear

KPIs need to be clear. Make sure the KPI can be easily understood to eliminate the potential for misunderstanding. Clarity will help keep all efforts on track to achieve the defined strategic objectives.

Focused

KPIs need to be focused on desired outcomes – the strategic objectives and mission of your organization. This ensures KPIs effectively support organizational goals.

Consider this example of a KPI. Suppose a CSF has been identified to improve customer satisfaction. An appropriate KPI to measure this CSF might be the percentage increase in the satisfaction rating on customer surveys.

If a CSF is to improve sales, then a plausible KPI to measure performance against it would be increase sales by a certain percentage over six months.

Suppose a team has identified a CSF to maintain a knowledgeable workforce. Measuring the decrease in employee turnover would be an appropriate KPI.

Question

What are the characteristics of effective KPIs?

Options:

1. They're relevant
2. They're quantifiable 3. They're clear
4. They're subjective
5. They're complex
6. They're focused

Answer

Option 1: This option is correct. Effective KPIs need to be relevant, meaning they support the organization's strategic objectives.

Option 2: This option is correct. KPIs quantify CSFs and therefore need to be quantifiable.

Option 3: This option is correct. Effective KPIs need to be clear so they can be understood by all those

involved. This helps ensure that all the work is contributing to what the organization wants to achieve.

Option 4: This option is incorrect. To be clear KPIs need to be objective, not open to interpretation.

Option 5: This option is incorrect. KPIs need to be detailed and clear, and should avoid being too complex. Otherwise they run the risk of being misunderstood.

Option 6: This option is correct. KPIs must be focused on making sure strategic objectives are achieved and thus support the organization's goals and mission.

Identifying a KPI with your team

Identifying a KPI with your team

A leader, Jonathan, and two team members, Kiley and Jose, are meeting to create effective KPIs for a project to improve high-speed Internet delivery to existing customers in rural areas. They're considering how the CSF to deliver reliable Internet service to rural customers can be measured.

Jonathan: We could measure the decrease in customer reports of outages over a one month period.

Jonathan is excited.

Kiley: Is that specific enough? Sometimes customers are offline and not aware the service is out.

Kiley is interested.

Jonathan: You're right. And some of them probably wouldn't even bother to report the outage because they assume it'll be restored soon.

Jonathan is impressed.

Jose: How about measuring the decrease in service failures in rural areas. Say over a month. And we could track this ourselves, using our own system.

Jose is confident.

Jonathan: Great work, guys. Are there any other KPIs we should use to measure this CSF?

Jonathan is encouraging.

In the previous conversation, Jonathan, Kiley, and Jose created a KPI to measure the CSF to deliver reliable Internet service to rural customers. The KPI created will measure any changes to service interruption, which is a direct performance indicator of reliable Internet service.

The KPIs can be quantified by tracking outages and measuring the percentage difference over a specified time period. The team will have to establish a benchmark to compare future measurements against.

The KPI clearly identifies what's being measured – Internet service failures in rural areas. Finally, to be effective the KPI must be focused on the CSF, and therefore one of the strategic objectives of the organization. In this case, the KPI supports the CSF by helping to quantify efforts to improve service delivery in rural areas.

Question

A company has set a strategic objective to increase customer loyalty. One CSF identified by the Customer Service Department is to satisfy customers. The department establishes several KPIs to help it measure progress toward this CSF.

Based on the specific situation, which KPIs are effective?

Options:

Performance Management

1. Number of customer complaints that remain unresolved at the end of a week
2. Percentage increase in repeat customers
3. Percentage increase in customer satisfaction ratings at year end
4. Decrease in the number of complaints
5. Number of new employees hired

Answer

Option 1: This option is correct. Directly related to customer satisfaction is the quick resolution of complaints. Tracking how many complaints remain unresolved at the end of a week can provide insight on whether customers are being satisfied.

Option 2: This option is correct. The number of customers who return to a company is a good indicator of satisfied customers.

Option 3: This option is correct. Knowing how customer satisfaction ratings have changed over the specified time range will help the unit understand if improvement is being made.

Option 4: This option is incorrect. This KPI fails to directly measure customer satisfaction. Customers may be dissatisfied but aren't complaining, so this isn't a useful KPI.

Option 5: This option is incorrect. This KPI doesn't measure something directly related to improving customer satisfaction.

Section 4 - Developing Role Profiles

Section 4 - Developing Role Profiles

Role profiles are the primary tool used to reach agreement on performance expectations between managers and the individuals who do the work.

Developing role profiles involves three steps. First, identify key results areas. These are the tasks that must be done well to perform the role.

Second, establish the technical competencies needed for the role. These might include educational qualifications.

Third, determine the behavioral competencies, or soft skills, required for the job.

Components of role profiles

Components of role profiles

Identifying critical success factors and establishing key performance indicators are the first two elements of planning for performance. The final element is to develop role profiles. Role profiles are used to define expectations so individual performance can be measured.

You can use a tool known as role profiling to define the jobs necessary to complete the work of your unit, team, or organization.

Because a partnership between managers and employees is essential to overall success, defining role profiles must also be a collaborative effort.

What's defined is the basis for a performance agreement between manager and employee. It also clarifies the expectations as a basis for measuring performance.

Sorin Dumitrascu

A role profile summarizes job requirements in three areas: key results, technical competencies, and behavioral competencies. Developing role profiles is essentially about answering questions in these three areas.

Key results areas

What are the key results expected from this job or role? This is the first question to answer. Here you are looking to identify the key results that need to be achieved for success in the role. For instance, milestones must be met for projects to be completed on time. Another example of a key results area may be to support underlying database infrastructure.

Technical competencies

Technical competencies need to be identified. You can guide your exploration by asking, "What are role holders expected to know and be able to do?" For example, does the role require an individual with a degree in business, database engineering, or programming?

Behavioral competencies

Each role also requires certain behavioral competencies. Ask "How are role holders expected to behave?" For instance, success in the role may require individuals to be able to communicate clearly and persuasively, contribute effectively on projects, or develop positive working relationships with colleagues.

In an existing performance management system, the same process can be used to update or verify existing role profiles.

Whenever it's used the point is the same – to clarify performance expectations and to ensure these expectations can be effectively monitored.

The process for defining roles is fairly straightforward, but requires some skill. Training from human resource specialists may be required for managers to develop the skills necessary to lead employees in developing role profiles.

Question

Which statements accurately describe role profiles?

Options:

1. Role profiles cover key results areas, technical competencies, and behavioral competencies
2. Role profiles are created by human resource personnel and managers
3. Role profiles are defined once and for all
4. Role profiles are used to define expectations so individual performance can be measured

Answer

Option 1: This option is correct. Role profiles define what individuals performing the role must accomplish, what they need to know, and how they need to behave.

Option 2: This option is incorrect. Role profiles are defined and agreed to by managers and the employee in the role.

Option 3: This option is incorrect. Existing role profiles can be updated to reflect changes to the role. This is typically done during performance reviews.

Option 4: This option is correct. Role profiles define performance expectations for individual employees.

Identifying key results areas

Identifying key results areas

The first thing you need to do to create a role profile is to identify the key results that need to be achieved for success in the role. This requires you to work with individual employees to determine the most important tasks involved, expectations for the work, and measures of success.

Xavier is a manager at a large multimedia company. He's meeting with Yolanda, an administrative assistant, to update her role profile. In this meeting, Xavier and Yolanda are discussing what she understands to be the key results areas of her job.

First, Xavier asks Yolanda to tell him about the most important tasks that are part of her job. Yolanda tells him that success in the role depends on her ability to provide administrative and logistical support to the directors and to make sure the department functions as it should.

Next, Xavier asks Yolanda to think about the support she provides directors and pick one task she's responsible for. Yolanda tells Xavier that part of her job is to help directors be productive.

Then, Xavier asks Yolanda to tell him how she measures success with this task. She explains that she feels she's succeeded in this when the directors have the resources and information they need.

Xavier and Yolanda continue to identify important tasks, expectations, and measures of success, until they have covered all the key tasks of her role.

Next, Xavier reviews what Yolanda has told him. He eliminates from the profile any information Yolanda has provided that isn't strictly relevant to her role.

For instance, Yolanda noted that she provides refreshments during team meetings. However, this isn't a duty she needs to perform as far as the department is concerned.

Xavier groups Yolanda's duties into three key results areas. These are secretarial and administrative support; projecting a professional and positive image of the department; and acting as liaison between the department and other functional areas, such as finance and translations. With Yolanda's agreement, he adds this information to the role profile.

Question

Jenna, a socio-economic specialist, has just described her job to her manager Karl. Access the learning aid Socio-economic Specialist to learn what she told Karl about what her job involves.

What are the critical responsibilities of this role?

Options:

1. Providing professional advice on all socio-economic matters related to the energy industry

2. Reviewing proposed projects and offering advice on them

3. Assisting in the site selection for energy projects

4. Helping to design the programs used to implement and assess projects

5. Reviewing the work of other specialists to assess it for accuracy and completeness

Answer

Option 1: This option is correct. Jenna has emphasized that providing advice is a very large part of her doing her job properly.

Option 2: This option is correct. Jenna has indicated that to effectively perform her role she must review proposed projects.

Option 3: This option is incorrect. Jenna doesn't select potential sites, but she does provide insight about the potential socio-economic impacts of them.

Option 4: This option is correct. Jenna has indicated that an important part of her job is helping to design the programs that are used to implement and assess the company's energy projects.

Option 5: This option is not correct. Jenna told Karl that her work is reviewed by a senior socio- economic specialist.

Defining technical competencies

Defining technical competencies

After identifying the key results areas of the role, you can define the required technical competencies. You'll have to ask certain questions to define technical competencies. First, what does the role holder need to be able to do or need to know to perform the role effectively?

The next question that needs to be answered is, what qualifications, technical and procedural knowledge, and skills does the holder need? For instance, is a business degree required? Or are planning, communication, and problem resolutions skills necessary?

The final question is designed to establish the performance expectation. For instance, how do you know when the role has been conducted well?

Recall the scenario with Xavier and Yolanda? Now that they've agreed to the key results areas, Xavier and

Yolanda meet to discuss the technical competencies required to do the job.

They begin again with supporting directors. Specific technical competencies for this key results area include a college diploma in secretarial studies and competency in the use of relevant computer applications. A final competency is to be bilingual.

Success also depends on Yolanda's ability to do certain things:

- write effective letters, memorandums, minutes, and reports,
- be professional in interpersonal relations, and use good manners, tact, diplomacy, and discretion,
- be reliable, self-directed, and flexible,
- employ excellent planning skills, and
- adapt to changing situations and manage stress effectively.

As Xavier and Yolanda work through each of the key results areas, they discover more technical competencies and add them to the role profile. They find that the technical competencies needed tend to apply to more than one key results area. Each technical competency is only recorded once in the role profile, to avoid duplication.

Question

Remember Jenna? She's the socio-economic specialist working with her manager, Karl, to create a role profile for her position.

What does the role require Jenna to know and be able to do?

Options:

1. Consistently apply appropriate principles and methods for socio-economic assessments

2. Demonstrate professional judgment and knowledge of a range of socio-economic matters

3. A degree in environmental science, rural planning, or other specialty related to socio-economic matters

4. Develop plans for socio-economic projects and organize the workloads of the project team

5. Interpret socio-economic project budgets in order to manage resources effectively within them

Answer

Option 1: This option is correct. Jenna must know and be able to apply the principles and methods of assessment.

Option 2: This option is correct. Jenna needs to be able to judge socio-economic matter to excel in her role.

Option 3: This option is correct. Jenna has a degree in environmental science. Without this knowledge she wouldn't be able to do her job.

Option 4: This option is incorrect. Like most individual employees, Jenna is responsible only for managing her own workload.

Option 5: This option is incorrect. Jenna sometimes provides input to budgets but she isn't responsible for project budgets.

Defining behavioral competencies

Defining behavioral competencies

The final step when developing a role profile is to define behavioral competencies, as you focus on the behavior needed to succeed. For instance, are personal drive, communication skills, customer focus, flexibility, or business awareness important to performance and success?

Behavioral competencies will differ from role to role. For instance, good communication skills won't be as important to a technician who works alone most of the time as they would be to a salesperson.

Xavier and Yolanda are ready to discuss the required behavioral competencies of the administrative assistant role. Several behavioral competencies are revealed as being necessary for Yolanda, or any other individual, to be successful in the role. These competencies involve communication, leadership, and teamwork.

Communication
Yolanda needs to communicate effectively and openly. This helps her ensure that messages are conveyed consistently and within context. She also needs to proactively participate in conversations.

Leadership
Yolanda must demonstrate leadership through integrity in all her actions and decisions. She must also treat everyone with respect and dignity.

Teamwork
Yolanda needs to demonstrate teamwork, build solid relationships, and anticipate and respond to the needs of others. She also needs to provide quality and efficiency driven solutions and services. And, she must align actions and decisions with external and internal clients' priorities.

Once role profiles have been created, it's useful to develop a way to measure performance. Based on the expectations set in role profiles, you can develop performance agreements with each employee.

These agreements provide standards for measuring employee performance. Typically used during appraisals, they provide a way to objectively summarize how well an employee is performing.

Question
Recall Jenna, the socio-economic specialist working with her manager, Karl, to create a role profile?

What personal skills does Jenna use to do her job well?

Options:
1. Establish good working relationships with team members and with colleagues in other teams

2. Recognize that team success is a shared responsibility and adds value to team results

3. Express honest and constructive points of view in writing

4. Work to set and meet challenging goals and seek ways to constantly improve work methods

5. Be driven to increase the volume of assessments completed for new customers

Answer

Option 1: This option is correct. Good working relationships are crucial to Jenna's performance.

Option 2: This option is correct. While Jenna often works alone, her efforts contribute to those of a team. She reveals that it's important in her role to put team work ahead of personal gain.

Option 3: This option is correct. Jenna reports that success in her job requires the ability to convey her opinions in a candid, but respectful, way.

Option 4: This option is incorrect. Jenna has very specific principles and methods to uphold while doing her job.

Option 5: This option is incorrect. Jenna isn't responsible for the volume of assessments to be completed or pursuing customers.

Updating a role profile

Updating a role profile

Harold is a manager at a customer support center. He's meeting with Molly, a customer care representative, to update her role profile. In this meeting, Harold and Molly are discussing her role, specifically what she understands to be the key results areas and the technical and behavioral competencies of her job.

Harold begins asking Molly about the key results areas of her position.

Harold: Tell me about the most important tasks that are part of your job. What's your top priority?

Harold is supportive.

Molly: Well, I'd say it's to satisfy the needs of my customers.

Molly is confident.

Harold: That sounds like the right attitude. But what do you have to do to keep customers satisfied?

61

Harold is interested.

Molly: Help resolve any issues they have with our products and services.

Molly is confident.

Harold: And how do you know you've succeeded?

Harold is interested.

Molly: When customers don't call again about the thing I helped them with.

Molly is confident.

Harold: That seems reasonable. And what personal traits would you say you rely on most when dealing with customers?

Harold is supportive.

Molly: Diplomacy and tact for sure! Patience and understanding come in handy too. Without them I'd have a hard time satisfying customers.

Molly is excited.

Harold: And what special knowledge do you need for your job?

Harold is interested.

Molly: My office technology diploma helped me learn the computer system more quickly, but on-the-job training helped the most.

Molly is reflective.

Harold has learned from Molly that one key results area of her role is satisfying customer needs. When it comes to technical competencies, Molly refers to her office technology diploma and the importance of on-the-job training. In this customer-centric role, Harold's not surprised that Molly emphasizes how vital behavioral competencies like diplomacy, tact, patience, and

Performance Management

understanding are. Harold adds this information to the role profile, once they've both agreed to it.

CHAPTER 2 - Monitoring and Improving Performance

CHAPTER 2 - Monitoring and Improving Performance

Section 1 - Setting Performance Targets
Section 2 - Monitoring Performance
Section 3 - Analyzing and Responding to Performance Gaps
Section 4 - Managing Underperformers

Section 1 - Setting Performance Targets
Section 1 - Setting Performance Targets

Setting targets and standards is the first stage of performance monitoring.

It's essential that all goals or objectives set are SMART – specific, measurable, achievable, relevant, and timely. The goal must be specific, with definite and clear aims that explicitly identify the criteria to be applied. It must also be measurable, meaning that it can be readily determined whether the goal has been achieved or not. The goal should be achievable – not beyond the scope of whoever it's assigned to. And the goal should be relevant to the organization's ultimate objectives. Finally, a date should be given for achieving the goal.

As well as being SMART, targets or goals should be consistent with employees' role profiles, and should support team and corporate objectives.

Monitoring and improving

Monitoring and improving

An effective performance management system involves five key phases. The first phase is to plan, which is mainly about establishing performance expectations. The second phase is to monitor performance levels, and phase three is to improve performance. Phase four is to review, which helps keep performance levels on track. The final phase is to reward, which incentivizes high performance. This course focuses on the second and third phases of performance management – monitoring and improving performance.

Monitoring and improving performance involves four steps. To monitor performance, you first set targets and standards, and then collect the performance data. To improve performance, analyze this performance data, and then respond to any performance gaps identified.

1. Set targets and standards

Monitoring performance begins with setting targets and standards.

Expectations must be made clear, and be consistent with employees' role profiles.

Any objectives set should support team and corporate goals. Finally, these objectives should be specific, measurable, achievable, relevant, and timely.

2. Collect performance data

The next step in monitoring performance is to collect performance data.

Decide first what information to gather, and then decide how to gather it and how often it should be gathered. Data collected should be organized and documented.

3. Analyze performance data

Improving performance begins with analyzing the performance data collected.

Analysis of the data involves comparing the results to targets to identify any performance gaps. Look for trends in the data, consider any fluctuations, assess whether the metrics applied are reasonable, and decide whether gaps need to be addressed.

4. Respond to performance gaps

The next step in improving performance is to respond to any performance gaps identified.

This means considering the potential causes of the gaps, deciding on appropriate solutions, and dealing with underperforming employees.

Question

Match each step of monitoring and improving performance to its relevant activity.

Options:

A. Set targets and standards
B. Collect performance data
C. Analyze performance data
D. Respond to performance gaps

Targets:

1. A manager clearly explains the expectations for employees' performance

2. After assessing the various options, a team leader decides how to gather performance data

3. A supervisor studies statistics on performance to determine if there are any trends

4. A manager investigates causes of performance gaps

Answer

Being clear about expectations is one aspect of setting targets and standards. The manager should also ensure expectations are consistent with employees' role profiles.

Deciding on how performance information should be gathered is one aspect of collecting the data. It's also necessary to decide what information to gather and how often to gather it.

Looking for trends in performance data gathered is one aspect of analyzing the data. It's also important to consider any fluctuations, assess whether the metrics applied are reasonable, and decide whether gaps need to be addressed.

Considering the potential causes of the gaps is one aspect of responding to performance gaps. The manager should also decide on appropriate solutions and deal with underperforming employees.

Setting targets and standards

Setting targets and standards

Setting targets and standards is an essential part of effective performance monitoring. When setting targets and standards, make sure that everyone knows what's expected. Above all else, any goals or objectives set must be SMART – specific, measurable, achievable, relevant, and timely.

Specific

Goals should be specific. This means setting definite and clear aims that explicitly identify the criteria to be applied.

Vague goals such as "provide better customer service" or "improve the delivery process" are too ambiguous, and don't give any firm indication of the aims.

However, when goals are specific, such as "reduce the number of customer complaints" or "increase the percentage of deliveries that are on time," the ultimate objective is easily understood.

Measurable

Results should be measurable so that you can readily determine whether goals have been achieved. Attach a precise number to the goal or target.

A baseline performance should also be identified against which future performance is measured. This could be previous data, current results, or the annual or industry average.

For example, "reduce employee turnover" isn't an easily measurable goal. Restating this goal as "reduce employee turnover by 10% on the 30% turnover recorded last year" makes it far easier to determine whether the goal has been achieved.

Achievable

It's important that goals are achievable. Goals should certainly be challenging, but not so challenging that there's little chance of them being achieved. Unachievable goals harm morale. But don't pitch them too low either – "easy" goals are meaningless.

Also be realistic about the number of goals you set. One SMART goal is better than two unachievable ones.

Relevant

Goals should be relevant to the aims and objectives of the organization. This ensures that goals set for individual employees are consistent with corporate goals.

When setting goals, it's important to confirm that they're clearly and explicitly aligned to broader team objectives, functional objectives, and corporate objectives.

Goals should also be consistent with the values and broader strategic direction of the organization.

Timely

Goals must be timely, with clear requirements about when they must be achieved. Unless there's a specific date set for accomplishing a particular goal, it may drag on indefinitely.

Don't frame a goal as, for example, "develop a new marketing plan." Instead, frame it as "develop a new marketing plan, with the first draft completed by February 1, management review conducted by February 20, and final draft approved by March 1."

This gives momentum to the process, and ensures progression.

As well as being SMART, targets or goals should be consistent with the key results areas in employees' role profiles. Role profiles detail employees' functions and responsibilities. You shouldn't set a target that clashes with some other aspect of that employee's role profile.

For example, an employee responsible for orchestrating a planned downsizing of the workforce shouldn't be given a goal of achieving a reduction in employee turnover. These tasks would be in direct conflict with one another. Similarly, don't set a goal that's irrelevant to that employee's main responsibilities.

Goals must also support team and corporate objectives. For example, if an organization's overall strategy is to aggressively build its brand profile, goals set for individual employees should be consistent with this. So it would be wrong to ask an employee to determine, for example, how the marketing budget could be slashed by 50%.

Consider the example of Reuben, the manager of a major organization's sales department. Reuben's department contains a new team that's responsible for identifying and developing new business leads. As part of the overall organization's strategy to significantly grow its sales, Reuben sets a specific goal for this team.

The team is to achieve 20% more leads than last year's average. Reuben makes everyone individually responsible for reaching this target. Reuben is confident that the goal is achievable because he knows it's the level routinely achieved by employees in the organization's best-performing competitor. He explains that everyone must achieve this level of performance within three months. Reuben has set effective targets and standards for his employees.

Increasing business leads is consistent with the new business development team members' role profiles, and it supports the organization's objective of growing sales. It's also SMART. As it's clear what's required and by how much, it's specific and measurable. It's achievable because this level of performance is being achieved by others within the industry. It's relevant because it's consistent with the overall organizational strategy to grow sales, and it's timely because it must be achieved within three months.

Question

Esther is the marketing manager of a cell phone handset manufacturer. Although her organization's handsets are superior in terms of design and build to its competitors' products, consumer research shows that this isn't recognized by consumers – just 14% of consumers recognize the brand's superiority. The organization wants to address this.

Esther asks Anneka, her senior marketing strategist, to devise a new marketing plan. She stresses the importance

Performance Management

of this task – telling her to be sure to create a compelling plan, no matter how long it takes.

In which ways has Esther effectively set this goal for Anneka?

Options:

1. The goal is timely and measurable
2. The goal is specific and achievable
3. The assignment is consistent with Anneka's role
4. The aim of the task matches the organization's objectives
5. The goal is relevant

Answer

Option 1: This option is incorrect. Esther hasn't given Anneka any time frame within which to achieve the goal, so it's not timely. Nor has she quantified the desired level of increase in consumer recognition of the brand's superiority, so it's not measurable.

Option 2: This option is incorrect. Esther hasn't told Anneka the specific aims of the new marketing plan – just given a vague instruction to devise a new plan. So it's not specific. And because Anneka hasn't been given this information, it's not achievable either.

Option 3: This option is correct. Targets or goals should be consistent with the key results areas in employees' role profiles. As a marketing strategist, Anneka would be responsible for developing a marketing plan.

Option 4: This option is correct. Esther's organization wants to more effectively communicate the superior quality of its products, so devising a marketing plan with this objective is consistent.

Option 5: This option is correct. The goal set for Anneka is consistent with the overall organizational objective, which makes it relevant.

Section 2 - Monitoring Performance
Section 2 - Monitoring Performance

When collecting performance data, first determine the data to be collected, and then determine how to collect the data.

When determining the data to be collected, follow what's obvious, get employees involved, focus on what's useful, and plan to gather data continuously.

There are four main methods that can be used to collect data: computer-generated reports, dashboards, surveys, and direct observation.

Collecting data

Collecting data

You can't monitor something without measuring it. Measuring requires data. And having set targets and standards, you next need to collect performance data. Managers must collect data and compare results to goals on a regular basis. They can then take action to help employees stay on track, or get back on track.

Performance management is about results. It's about asking, "Have goals been met?" And if not, "Why not?" But don't just analyze results. Look at the process that led to the results. This gives insight into why and how the results came about. It's always useful to ask, "Can the process be improved?"

There are two steps to collecting performance data. The first is to determine the data to be collected. The second step is to determine how to collect the data.

Determining data to collect

Determining data to collect

There are four principles to follow when it comes to determining the data to collect. First, follow what's obvious by collecting data suggested by established SMART goals where possible. Second, get employees involved in the process. Third, make sure the data you collect is really useful. And, finally, plan to collect data continuously.

Follow what's obvious

If you have created SMART goals, the data you need to collect should be obvious.

For example, if you've set a goal of reducing customer complaints by 25%, you need data on the number of complaints received.

Get employees involved

Solicit employee input when deciding what data to collect.

Involving employees in the process fosters a sense of ownership and helps employees be more self-managing.

Make sure data is useful

There's an unlimited amount of data that could be collected. Don't waste time collecting useless information. Having a small amount of data that you'll use is far better than having so much that you can't use it all.

Just because data is interesting or novel doesn't necessarily make it useful.

Plan to collect data continuously

Plan to gather data continuously and in a systematic way, not randomly or sporadically or at the last minute.

Performance monitoring is an ongoing process, so data collection should be ongoing too.

If you leave data collection to the last minute, there's a risk that the data needed won't be available or that there won't be enough time for proper collection and analysis.

For example, Arlene is the manger of the Accounting Department of an organization that supplies food retailers with materials.

She recently implemented procedural changes as part of a project to reduce invoicing errors. Before these measures, 7% of invoices contained errors. She establishes a SMART goal of reducing invoicing errors to 3% within six months.

She intends to collect data on the invoice error rate for each week. She hopes to identify trends that give insight into the effectiveness of the changes implemented, and to monitor improvements in the error rate.

She speaks with the departmental employees involved in invoicing to get their views on the program.

She learns that invoices to overseas retailers, which involve different currencies, are particularly prone to error. With this insight, she arranges for the error rate for these invoices to be collected separately to enable closer monitoring.

One of Arlene's employees suggests contacting every retailer that has purchased from the organization during the last two years to ask for feedback on the invoicing process.

Arlene recognizes that this could produce some interesting insights, but doesn't think the information would be overly important.

She also knows it would require a great number of resources to process and analyze this information. As these resources aren't available, the idea is impractical.

In deciding on the information to collect, Arlene follows the obvious by focusing on invoicing error rates. She also ensures that the required data is collected systematically and continuously. She involves employees, and gains an important insight from doing so. Finally, when assessing the options, she focuses on usefulness over availability, accepting there's no point collecting data that won't or can't be used.

Question

Which examples indicate an effective approach to determining data to collect when monitoring performance?

Options:

1. When monitoring a cost-cutting initiative, Keith collects data on each department's monthly costs

2. Erica involves her employees in deciding what data to collect

3. Sam doesn't collect historical data as he knows he won't use it

4. Chavondra collects data at the end of each month during the six-month program to increase efficiency

5. Omar regards it as his sole responsibility to decide what data to collect

6. As part of the drive to increase profits, Natasha collects all available data on the organization's operations

Answer

Option 1: This option is correct. When deciding what data to collect, follow what's obvious. In Keith's case, the need for data on costs is self-evident.

Option 2: This option is correct. Erica is right to solicit employee input when deciding what data to collect. Doing this increases ownership of the management process and fosters self-management.

Option 3: This option is correct. When deciding on the data to collect, focus on what's useful. Sam is correct not to waste resources collecting data that won't be used.

Option 4: This option is correct. Data should be collected continuously, not occasionally. Chavondra is right to gather data systematically and on an ongoing basis.

Option 5: This option is incorrect. When deciding the data to collect, it's important to solicit employee input so that employees have more of a sense of ownership of the performance management process.

Option 6: This option is incorrect. Only data that is useful should be gathered. Collecting whatever's available, irrespective of use, is wasteful.

Reports and dashboards

Reports and dashboards

The second step when collecting performance data is to determine how to collect the data. Methods of collection include computer-generated reports, dashboards, employee surveys, customer surveys, and direct observation.

Computer-generated reports are one way of collecting data. Most organizations have many reports on issues such as sales, costs, and revenues. But it's important to avoid information overload – too much information can be as useless as too little. Before generating a report, consider what's already available, and consider the time it will take to create and review the report.

Consider what's available

Because of the likely volume of reports already produced, consider what's available before creating a new one.

There's no point duplicating or adding to an already unmanageable load. Check first whether the required information already exists somewhere else.

For example, an operations manager who needs information on the organization's cost structure may find that the organization's Finance Department already has detailed information at hand.

Consider time to create and review

Consider the time required to create reports. Reports tend to be regular and reoccurring, such as monthly sales reports. The value of reports often depends on how quickly and frequently they can be created.

For example, if there is a month between sales reports and it takes a week to review the report, the review will be dealing with some information that is already five weeks old. The usefulness of such information may be questionable. Highly detailed reports may take even longer to review, which may further reduce their timeliness.

Dashboards are another option for collecting data. Dashboards are interfaces that visually present information to facilitate effective performance management. They enable users to monitor a range of selected data and metrics at a glance. Effective dashboards include relevant key performance indicators, feature actionable information, cater to different needs, and aren't overloaded with information.

Include key performance indicators

Determine the relevant key performance indicators, and include these in the dashboard.

Defining the relevant indicators depends on what's being measured. For example, key indicators for an organization that's measuring its success in growing its customer base might be new customers added, number of customers lost, and status of existing customers.

Feature actionable information

Because a dashboard is purely a means to an end, it should only feature actionable information – in other words, information that facilitates action toward the stated goals and objectives.

For example, consider a dashboard created to present data to measure progress in reducing cost. Actionable information would be data on the costs incurred by various activities in comparison with the contribution these activities make to profitability. This information provides clear insight into where cost-cutting actions should be focused.

Cater to different needs

Different departments and individuals within an organization need different information, and dashboards must cater to these different needs.

When creating a dashboard, consider the various needs and interests. Ensure that all the information relevant to all users is provided. As well as providing data diversity, incorporate functions that enable users to customize what they see.

For example, users should be able to deselect or "hide" data that's not relevant to them.

Aren't overloaded with information

Don't overload the dashboard with information. An effective dashboard is simple and uncluttered. Making excessive use of bright colors or gimmicks frustrates users, and reduces the value and appeal of the dashboard.

Surveys

Surveys

Employee surveys are another way of collecting data. They provide information on issues such as morale, the working environment, processes and procedures, and training needs. Findings help you analyze performance and uncover problems. Surveys should be conducted regularly over an extended period of time, so you can compare results.

For example, Rico, an organization's **HR** manager, is monitoring the performance of an initiative designed to reduce employee turnover. He surveys the employees to determine general feelings towards the organization.

The results show that most employees are satisfied with pay levels but unhappy with the working environment and the quality of training offered.

For an organization attempting to reduce costs, an employee survey could indicate the processes and procedures that cause inefficiencies – and increase costs. Employees often have the best insight into the sources of bottlenecks, delays, and waste.

When considering employee surveys, assess your need for the information against the time required to gather it. Employee surveys aren't a fast method of collecting information.

It can take months to develop and conduct a survey, compile and evaluate the results, and then implement responsive action. It's usually necessary to repeat the survey around a year later to enable comparison.

Another method of collecting data is through customer surveys. These give interesting insights into how your customers rate your organization's products or services. Customers are generally keen to provide feedback – but must be asked. Options include mystery shopping, customer comment cards, and telephone surveys.

Mystery shopping

Mystery shopping is a method of recording the customer experience. Mystery shoppers are individuals employed to pose as real customers – purchasing products, asking questions, or making complaints – and then report back on the experience. Because the organization's employees don't know that the "customer" is really a mystery shopper, it's assumed that the experience is typical. This gives the organization a real sense of how customers are being treated.

Comment cards

Customer comment cards are preprinted cards that invite customers to rate their satisfaction with the product or service provided. When the comments and ratings are collated, they provide a good overview of how customers rate the organization.

Telephone surveys

Organizations can use telephone surveys to follow up with customers and solicit feedback on their experiences. They differ from other forms of surveys because the organization's representative can ask specific questions in response to customers' comments or replies.

Question

Which statements are true of data collection methods?

Options:

1. Before creating a computer-generated report, ensure the information isn't already available

2. Employee surveys are a relatively slow method of collecting data

3. Customer surveys can provide insight into how customers rate an organization's services

4. Dashboards should feature information that facilitates action toward the organization's objectives

5. The value of a computer-generated report increases in line with the time invested in creating it

6. The main difficulty with customer surveys is that customers tend to be reluctant to participate

Answer

Option 1: This option is correct. Most organizations have lots of existing reports. There's no point duplicating them.

Option 2: This option is correct. It can take months to develop an employee survey, conduct it, compile and evaluate the results, and then act on the results.

Option 3: This option is correct. Customer surveys can provide information about how customers view an organization's offerings.

Option 4: This option is correct. A dashboard is a means to an end, and so should feature actionable information.

Option 5: This option is incorrect. The value of a computer-generated report depends on how quickly

Direct observation

Direct observation

The direct observation method of collecting data is useful when performance is unsatisfactory, but the reasons are unknown. There are advantages and disadvantages. It's simple to use, and provides firsthand information. However, it's time consuming, and may distort employee performance because the employees are aware they're being observed. It may also be unsuitable for primarily mental activities.

Direct observation involves several activities. Prepare yourself, develop observation forms, and prepare employees. To make the most of direct observation, you should also interview employees, and ensure you observe more than once.

Prepare yourself

Prepare yourself by deciding the focus of the observation. Be selective because direct observation can be time consuming. Focus on one or two central issues.

Then divide the activities being monitored into subcomponents. For example, observe how employees greet customers, discuss the customers' needs, make recommendations, and conduct the payment process.

These subcomponents can be further divided into tasks and subtasks. For example, when employees recommend products to customers, do they suggest alternatives and communicate their respective benefits?

Develop observation forms

Developing observation forms helps standardize observations, ensures all important areas are covered, and enables efficient aggregation of the collected data.

Compile a list of the issues to be observed, leaving spaces for recording the observations. To maximize objectivity and minimize observer variation, use closed response categories. Also, leave space for additional observations.

Prepare employees

Prepare employees by explaining the reasons for the observation. Be open and honest about these reasons.

Make it clear the purpose of the observation is to help improve employee performance, not to be judgmental.

Prior to the actual observation, develop rapport with whoever's being observed. Previous contact can alleviate the anxiety that often occurs when people are being observed.

Interview employees

Interview employees to collect information that wasn't collected through the observation.

Ask employees to clarify anything that wasn't understood during the observation. Also ask if there's anything significant that was missed.

Employees often have better insight into procedures and process than management, and can help identify problems before they become severe.

Observe more than once

To ensure you have a proper sample for generalization, observe more than once.

Single observations can be misleading as people tend to behave differently when under observation.

When observations last longer and are repeated, employees become less self-conscious and act more naturally.

Consider the example of Abby, the production manager of a manufacturing organization. Abby's organization is aiming to increase production by 20%. Data shows that its manufacturing facility operates at just 75% capacity, despite being fully resourced. Abby doesn't know why it isn't operating at full capacity.

She decides to use direct observation. She hopes to identify the processes and procedures that are obstructing productivity.

She limits the scope of the intended observation to this, ignoring things such as employee morale and adherence to safety standards.

To direct her observation, Abby compiles a detailed observation form. This lists the components of two activities: processing of raw materials and quality control. She believes these are the main bottlenecks in the production process.

She meets with the facility's employees in advance of the initial observation. She explains what the observation will entail and its aims, making it clear that her intention is to identify problems and to help employees improve the overall process.

Abby observes the employees for three hours on the first day, and repeats the observation every two or three days for three weeks.

She notices that many employees are very conscious of her presence on the first two or three occasions, but they relax and behave more naturally after that.

At the end of the observation process, Abby has made an interesting discovery – that each employee stops production every 30 minutes to fill in paperwork, which is then brought to the production office. This takes around 10 minutes.

Abby speaks directly with the employees, and learns that this is a formal requirement that predates the computerization of the facility's internal process. Everyone agrees that it serves no practical purpose, and there's uncertainty as to why it has never been changed.

Abby has made good use of direct observation. She first decided the focus of the observation, and developed an effective observation form on the basis of this decision. She then prepared the employees by meeting with them and explaining the reasons for the observation. She observed on several occasions to ensure she had a reliable sample for generalization, and then interviewed the employees for clarification of the reasons behind her findings.

Question

Which guidelines on the direct observation method of collecting data are correct?

Options:

1. Decide the specific aspects of behavior to be observed

2. Create an observation form with space to record observations

3. Be honest about the aims of the observation exercise

4. Discuss findings with employees to clarify any doubts

5. Observe for a sufficient amount of time over a sufficient period

6. Allow the observer to decide what's observed

7. Explain that continued employment depends on employees impressing the observer

Answer

Option 1: This option is correct. It's important to prepare yourself for direct observation, which includes deciding the observation's focus.

Option 2: This option is correct. It's necessary to develop an observation form, which includes the issues being observed and spaces for recording observations.

Option 3: This option is correct. Preparing employees includes explaining the reasons for the observation, which should be honest and open.

Option 4: This option is correct. It's useful to interview employees to clarify things that weren't understood.

Option 5: This option is correct. To ensure you have a proper sample for generalization, it's necessary to observe for extended periods and more than once.

Option 6: This option is incorrect. Preparing means deciding in advance what's to be observed, and sticking to

Performance Management

this. Because observation can be time consuming, selectivity is essential.

Option 7: This option is incorrect. It should be clearly explained to employees that the aim is to identify problems, not evaluate their individual performances.

Section 3 - Analyzing and Responding to Performance Gaps

Improving performance is the third phase of the performance management process. There are two steps involved: analyze the performance data and respond appropriately to any performance gaps identified.

When analyzing performance data, determine whether a performance gap exists, determine if there's a need for action, and identify the causes of the gap.

When responding to performance gaps, first determine whether expectations are clear and understood. Then check if feedback is being provided, that the employees have the required knowledge and skill to reach the target, that there's a willingness to succeed in this, and that no other task is preventing employees from reaching their target.

Analyzing data

Analyzing data

Once targets have been set and data collected to monitor performance, it's time to focus on improving performance. This is the third phase in the performance management process. It involves two tasks: analyze the performance data and respond appropriately to any performance gaps identified.

There are three steps to analyzing performance data. First, determine whether there is a performance gap. If there is, determine if there's a need for action – is it worth intervening? If it is, identify the causes of the gap.

The first step is to determine whether a performance gap exists. To do this, compare the actual performance results to previously set targets. It's also useful to look for trends in the collected data.

Compare results to targets

You can determine whether a performance gap exists by comparing performance results to performance targets.

A performance gap exists when there's a difference between actual performance and targeted performance.

For example, if an employee is handling 20 calls per shift, despite having a target of 35, there's clearly a performance gap.

Look for trends

Look for trends in the collected data when determining if a performance gap exists as this shows how performance is faring over time.

If the performance gap is narrowing over time, it's at least trending in the right direction, and progress is being made.

Also, a certain amount of fluctuation in performance levels is normal, and doesn't necessarily indicate a performance gap. So long as the "gap" is within the range of normal fluctuation, it's not a problem.

For instance, if a sales team doesn't achieve its sales target during a period of exceptionally low demand, this suggests the product or service is seasonal – not a performance gap.

The second step is to decide if intervention is appropriate. Not all performance gaps require intervention. The employee responsible for achieving the performance level may have identified the gap, and may already be acting to address or eliminate it. Provide assistance if necessary, but allow the employee to take responsibility for performance. Promoting employee self-management is an important part of effective performance management.

Performance Management

But intervention is required if you can answer any of these questions in the affirmative. Is the performance gap having a negative impact elsewhere in the organization or obstructing other employees' efforts to achieve their goals? Is the gap likely to worsen if it's ignored? Would ignoring it send the wrong message about the importance of goals? Or is this gap indicative of a wider performance problem?

Consider the example of Dominique, the customer relations manager of an online retail organization that wants to improve its reputation for customer service. The initiative involves a range of functions, including complaint handling, processing of returns and refunds, order processing, and delivery.

The aim is to improve all of these functions to provide better service to customers. The initiative is being backed by an extensive marketing campaign designed to promote the organization as a customer- focused retailer.

The general performance is good, with interim targets being either met or exceeded. The only exception is deliveries. Just 60% of deliveries were on time this month. This is far short of the 90% target, and also represents a fall from the previous month, when 70% were on time.

Dominique recognizes the need for intervention to address this obvious performance gap. Having gone from 70 to 60%, it's trending in the wrong direction and may get worse. The team responsible for deliveries appears unaware of the situation. Dominique's concerned about the negative impact on other's work – the Marketing Department is promoting the organization as being customer-centered, but delivery performance doesn't back this up. She also knows that ignoring this problem would send the wrong message to other employees.

Question

In which instances should a manager definitely act to address a performance gap?

Options:

1. Without any extenuating circumstances, sales are 20% below the targeted level

2. Over recent months, the number of faulty products has increased from 8% to 14%

3. An employee who's severely underperforming is unaware of the situation

4. The failure to control costs is stretching the organization's budget and leaving employees under-resourced

5. Although it's an isolated problem that will resolve itself in time, the gap will affect the fourth quarter profit margin

6. Costs are 25% above the targeted level due to temporary staff recruitment during a busy period

Answer

Option 1: This option is correct. When there's a difference between actual performance and targeted performance, a performance gap exists. Unless it's clearly temporary, this gap should be addressed.

Option 2: This option is correct. It's important to look for trends when analyzing performance data. A widening performance gap means it's trending in the wrong direction, so needs to be addressed.

Option 3: This option is correct. Intervention might not be necessary in situations where the relevant employee has already identified the gap and begun acting to address it. Where this isn't the case, intervention is necessary.

Option 4: This option is correct. When a performance gap is having a negative impact elsewhere in the organization and obstructing the work of other employees, intervention is necessary.

Option 5: This option is incorrect. When a performance gap isn't indicative of a wider performance problem and won't likely worsen if not dealt with, intervention isn't strictly necessary.

Option 6: This option is incorrect. When there's a good reason behind the failure to reach targets, it shouldn't necessarily be deemed a performance gap. In this situation, intervention isn't required.

If it's decided that a performance gap does require action, it's necessary to identify the exact causes of the gap. This is the third step. To do this, ask, "What's behind the performance gap?" Also ask, "Is the metric or target still relevant?"

What's behind the gap?

Determine what's behind the gap by identifying and examining any factors or events that might have caused it.

When performance isn't as expected, it's often possible to pinpoint something unusual or something that changed during the period.

Factors could be the introduction of a new process or technology, or a lack of adequate instruction, feedback, skill, or motivation.

Is metric still relevant?

When trying to identify the causes of the gap, consider whether the metric or target is still relevant. It may be out of date or need to be reconsidered.

If any of the underlying factors or conditions that influence performance has changed, it may be necessary to adjust the performance target.

For example, when Dominique investigates delivery time failures, she finds that deliveries are being delayed by a newly introduced process.

As part of the effort to improve customer service, the delivery team is now required to double-check all orders for accuracy before shipment.

The team hasn't been given any additional resources to match its expanded role. This is what's causing the delays.

Now that she's discovered the cause of the performance gap, Dominique considers whether the target is still relevant. She needs to honestly assess whether the delivery team can be expected to make 90% of deliveries on time without any extra resources when the delivery process has been made lengthier.

Question

Having decided that action is needed to address a failure to achieve a targeted 20% cut in costs, what would be appropriate questions to ask?

Options:

1. "Have there been any process changes introduced that obstructed efforts to achieve the target?"

2. "Is the target of 20% still feasible under current conditions?"

3. "What measures could be introduced to better motivate employees to achieve the target?"

4. "Can overall organizational objectives be achieved without the targeted reduction in costs?"

Answer

Option 1: This option is correct. Trying to determine what's behind the performance gap begins with identifying and examining any factors or events that might have caused it.

Option 2: This option is correct. Performance gaps often emerge because the target is no longer relevant, perhaps due to changes in underlying factors or conditions.

Option 3: This option is incorrect. This approach wouldn't provide any direct insight into the reasons for the gap, which should be the aim once it's been deemed necessary to intervene.

Option 4: This option is incorrect. The aim should be to determine the reasons for the performance gap. Simply accepting the gap would be entirely inappropriate.

Responding to gaps

Responding to gaps

After analyzing the performance data, the second task when improving performance is to respond to performance gaps. Start by asking, "Are expectations clear?" A performance gap may be due to an employee not understanding what's expected in terms of quality, quantity, or timeliness. To clarify expectations, set goals and standards. If expectations are already clear, check whether there's enough feedback. If not, give feedback and direction.

If feedback has already been provided, ask "does the performer have the required knowledge and skill?" If not, provide mentoring or training. If this isn't the problem, consider whether the performer's willing to do the job. If not, either change the performer or reassign the responsibility. If the willingness is there, ask "is another task interfering with efforts to perform adequately?" If this is the case, remove that other task.

Consider again the example of Dominique, the customer relations manager of the online retail organization that's aiming to improve its reputation for customer service. She's now beginning her response to the organization's delivery team's failure to achieve the target for on-time deliveries.

She knows that the target of 90% of deliveries on time was made clear to the delivery team. She confirms that this target was an explicit part of the overall initiative to improve customer service. There's no need for this goal to be communicated.

She also knows feedback has been provided regularly, at the beginning of the initiative and at monthly intervals since then. Dominique personally chaired a meeting last month to discuss how the team could increase the then rate of 70% to the target of 90%.

She's also confident that the team has all the necessary skills and knowledge to achieve the target. It's an experienced team that expressed confidence at the outset of the initiative in its ability to perform to the required level. Additional training isn't necessary.

Dominique has no doubt that the team is willing to do the job. It's been an enthusiastic supporter of the initiative from the beginning. There's no question of there being a need to replace employees or reassign the responsibility.

This confirms to Dominique that the problem is task interference. It's clear to her now that being required to double-check orders for accuracy before shipment is interfering with the team's ability to get deliveries made on time. The remedy is to reassign this task to the shipment packing team.

Case Study: Question 1 of 2
Scenario

Justin is the operations manager of a regional passenger airline that's developing a reputation for regular delays to its flights.

This is having a negative impact on customer satisfaction, employee morale, and sales. Despite a long-standing organizational commitment to sustaining an "on time" rate of 90%, last year's rate was just

75%. For the first quarter of this year, it was 70%.

Justin has developed a detailed plan to improve performance. It requires all relevant functions – passenger check-in, baggage handling, passenger boarding, aircraft maintenance, and between-flight safety check – to improve the efficiency of their respective processes.

Assess how Justin should analyze and respond to a performance gap. Answer the questions in order.

Question

One month into the plan, new data shows that the efficiency of every function, with the exception of between-flight safety check, has improved.

Under what circumstances should Justin intervene to address this performance gap?

Options:

1. Every time it takes longer than expected, the passenger boarding process is delayed

2. Other teams are becoming complacent, having seen that inefficiencies are still tolerated

3. Although this particular gap isn't responsible for delaying flights, there's no sound justification for it

4. The safety check team manager is extremely concerned about the gap, and has developed a plan to address it

5. There have been problems with the management of the flight check team before

Answer

Option 1: This option is correct. The performance gap needs to be addressed because it's affecting another function, and preventing the passenger boarding team from achieving its target.

Option 2: This option is correct. Not addressing this performance gap sends the wrong message about the importance of the overall initiative. For this reason, intervention is essential.

Option 3: This option is incorrect. Intervention isn't essential as the performance gap isn't overly important. It isn't obstructing the overall pursuit of the target.

Option 4: This option is incorrect. As the employee responsible for achieving the performance level has identified the gap and is acting to address it, intervention isn't necessary.

Option 5: This option is correct. One legitimate reason for intervening is when the gap may be indicative of a wider performance problem.

Case Study: Question 2 of 2

Justin decides to intervene and discusses the situation with Joel, the manager of the safety check team.

Joel explains that his team members are fully aware that they're regularly missing the target set for them, and are doing their best to improve. However, he reminds Justin that many of his team members are new employees, and that the process is often stalled when they need to consult more experienced employees.

He also tells Justin that because safety teams must, in accordance with company policy, get each check signed off by the on-duty supervisor, there are inevitable delays during particularly busy periods.

What actions might Justin take to address the safety team's performance gap?

Options:

1. Ensure comprehensive training is given to all new employees to ensure they can perform independently

2. Change company policy to permit other qualified team members to sign off on checks

3. Ensure everyone understands that checks must be completed within 30 minutes

4. Recruit new employees to replace any existing employee who's underperforming

Answer

Option 1: This option is correct. The performance gap is partly attributable to some employees lacking the required skills to perform their roles. These employees need to be better trained.

Option 2: This option is correct. The policy that the supervisor must sign off all checks is interfering with the safety team's ability to achieve its target. In situations where a task is interfering in this way, it should be removed.

Option 3: This option is incorrect. Setting goals and standards is appropriate when expectations are not fully understood. However, this isn't the case with Joel's team.

Option 4: This option is incorrect. Replacing employees is an appropriate action when there's an unwillingness to do what's required to reach the target. However, this isn't the case with Joel's team.

Section 4 - Managing Underperformers

There are four steps to dealing with an underperformer.

First, identify and agree on the problem. This involves analyzing the employee's performance data. Second, establish the cause of the problem through factual analysis. Third, decide and agree on an action plan, which should include concrete goals and the required actions for achieving them. Last, provide the resources needed by the employee to achieve the performance target, and follow up to ensure progress is being made.

Initial steps

Initial steps

As you strive to monitor and improve performance, you'll likely have to deal with underperformers. Managing underperformers should be a positive process. This means celebrating success, addressing failures constructively, and viewing mistakes as opportunities for improvement. There are four steps to dealing with an underperformer: identify and agree on the problem, establish the cause of the problem, decide and agree on an action plan, and provide the necessary resources and follow up.

Identifying and agreeing on the problem is the first step to managing an underperforming employee. This process depends on employee awareness of personal performance targets, metrics applied, and actual performance data. Being able to show how the performance data compares to known targets and standards will help you reach agreement with the employee about the performance gap. And this is where you need to start.

For example, if an employee, who's required to sell 100 units of product per month, sells an average of just 40 units, it's easy to identify and agree on the problem.

This is because the performance target, the metric applied, and the actual performance are clearly apparent.

Establishing the cause of the problem is your second step when managing an underperformer. Instead of attaching blame or making accusations, you need to identify the facts and then determine the reasons.

Identify the facts

Identifying the facts behind underperformance is an essential part of establishing the cause.

This should be a joint effort between manager and employee.

An effective decision about how to manage the situation can only come from factual analysis.

Determine the reasons

When determining the reasons, distinguish between external and internal factors.

External factors are outside the control of the employee, such as reduced consumer demand due to an economic downturn. Internal factors are within the employee's control, such as reduced productivity due to a lack of punctuality.

Perhaps the employee hasn't been given enough support, guidance, or training. Or the employee might not understand what's expected. It could also be that the employee lacks ability and can't do the job. Or perhaps the underperformance stems from a lack of knowledge or a poor attitude.

Performance Management

Agreeing on an action plan is the third step in managing underperformance. An action plan should lay out clear, measurable goals, and state the required actions for achieving them. It should be developed in partnership between manager and employee. It involves the employee taking action to improve performance, and the manager providing support, advice, and guidance. It's essential that both understand how success will be measured.

An action plan could include the following:
- commitment from the employee to improve skills or alter behavior,
- agreement from the employee that a change in attitude is required, or
- commitment from the manager to give better support or guidance.

Question

Should the process of developing an action plan primarily be driven by the employee, the manager, or both?

Options:
1. Employee
2. Manager
3. Both

Answer

An action plan should be developed in partnership between employee and manager.

Meeting with an under-performer

Meeting with an under-performer

Now that you've learned about the initial steps to take when dealing with underperformance, consider the example of Alvin and Pamela. Alvin is the managing director of a manufacturing organization. Three months ago, he assigned Pamela the task of reducing the defect rate in the organization's manufactured output. They agreed a target of 2%, compared to the initial rate of 7%. Reviewing the current data, Alvin's unhappy that the defect rate has remained at 7%.

Follow along as Alvin and Pamela discuss the most recent performance data.

Alvin: When we started this project, we agreed on a 2% target, right? But we're still at 7%.

Pamela: I know. And I know you can't be happy with that.

Alvin: And puzzled. Where's the problem?

Pamela: Well, I tried tracking the defects but that hasn't reduced them. I don't really know what else to do.

Alvin: In these situations, you have to intervene earlier. Define the inspection sample process...make sure defective products don't reach the production line.

Pamela: That makes sense. I guess I didn't have the experience to realize that! Maybe I need to get more advice when it comes to these tasks...

Alvin: I can help there! Let's set up a formal structure of cooperation and guidance. You just need to be pointed in the right direction, right?

Pamela: Yeah, great! I think that would really help.

Early in the meeting, Alvin identified the specific problem surrounding Pamela's underperformance. He did this by restating the performance target, and comparing this to the actual performance data.

He then established the cause of the problem, which was pinpointed as being Pamela's lack of experience.

Finally, Alvin formulated an action plan with Pamela's involvement. The plan will see Alvin providing guidance, assistance, and support.

Support and follow up

Support and follow up

Providing resources and follow-up is the final step in managing an underperforming employee. Support the employee's implementation of the action plan by providing necessary training, guidance, or resources. And be sure to monitor the employee's progress toward reaching the performance target and discuss any additional actions that might be required.

For example, say you have employees who are underperforming because they lack the necessary skills. You could put in place a training program to help them develop these skills.

A manager could arrange to meet regularly with an underperforming employee to review progress, and provide any required assistance.

Providing feedback to an underperforming employee gives a greater sense of direction and builds confidence.

Performance Management

Question

Leroy, the general manager of a major hotel, has developed a strategy to grow revenues from corporate business by 40% as part of an overall drive to boost profits. This requires a significant increase in the number of corporate functions and conferences hosted by the hotel. The hotel has the capacity to host 24 such events each month, but last year hosted an average of just 10 per month.

Six months ago, Leroy set Elizabeth, the hotel's corporate business manager, the target of increasing this average to 20 per month within 12 months. They agreed to review progress after six months, and set an interim target of 15 per month for this point.

When he analyzes the data to assess Elizabeth's six-month progress, he's disappointed that there's been no increase. He meets with Elizabeth to discuss her underperformance.

What would be appropriate comments to make to effectively manage Elizabeth's underperformance?

Options:

1. "We should be at 15 per month by now, but we haven't moved off 10."

2. "What do you think has prevented you from reaching the target?"

3. "So it's agreed: you'll be more proactive, and I'll make myself available for brainstorming sessions."

4. "We'll meet weekly to review progress from now on, and I'll assign Frank to assist you."

5. "The bottom line is that you've made no progress whatsoever in six months. That's unacceptable."

6. "I appreciate this isn't an easy task, but you'll just have to try harder to reach the target."

Answer

Option 1: This option is correct. Effectively managing underperformance must begin by identifying and agreeing on the problem. Leroy has done this by describing the shortfall between Elizabeth's performance and the agreed target.

Option 2: This option is correct. Effective management of underperformance requires a manager to establish the cause of the problem. In asking this question, Leroy is involving Elizabeth in determining the facts.

Option 3: This option is correct. Agreeing on an action plan is an important step in managing underperformance. Leroy and Elizabeth have agreed that she needs to adjust her behavior and approach, and he needs to provide more support.

Option 4: This option is correct. Providing resources and following up is an essential aspect of effectively managing underperformance. Leroy's doing this by agreeing to monitor progress and provide additional support.

Option 5: This option is incorrect. Instead of blaming or criticizing, a manager should try to establish the cause of the performance gap.

Option 6: This option is incorrect. When dealing with underperformance, a manager should support the employee's implementation of the action plan with training, guidance, and resources.

CHAPTER 3 - Reviewing and Rewarding Performance

CHAPTER 3 - Reviewing and Rewarding Performance

Section 1 - Rating Performance
Section 2 - Appraising Performance
Section 3 - Conducting a Performance Appraisal Meeting
Section 4 - Rewarding Performance

Section 1 - Rating Performance

Section 1 - Rating Performance

An effective performance management system links the management of an organization's human resources to its mission, corporate objectives, and strategic planning initiatives.

Performance appraisal involves evaluating each employee's performance to determine that person's value to the organization. Rating scales provide an equitable method of assessing an employee's overall performance and output.

Rating scales show how well the employee is meeting predetermined standards – the criteria against which the performance is measured.

The performance management system

The performance management system

An effective performance management system is an essential tool for the development of a productive workforce. It records management expectations and how well an individual has met those expectations. It also gives management a practical method to align employee efforts with the organization's mission and strategic goals. Performance management also provides a straightforward rationale for appraising and compensating employees fairly.

Performance management is an ongoing process with five phases – plan, monitor, improve, review, and reward. Each phase is essential to help employees understand what's expected of them in their jobs and how their performance relates to the success of the organization as a whole.

The first phase is plan, which is mainly about establishing the employee's performance expectations. The second phase is monitor, which means collecting relevant performance data to compare to those expectations. The third phase is improve, which involves analyzing that data and identifying improvement opportunities. The fourth phase is review, when results of the assessment are presented to the employee. The fifth and final phase is reward, where the employee's performance appraisal is tied in to the organization's reward system.

The performance management process is an effective way of establishing and maintaining communication between managers and employees. This course deals with the final two phases of the performance management process: reviewing and rewarding performance.

Question

Which statements best describe the purpose of performance management?

Options:

1. Establishing and maintaining communication between managers and employees

2. Documenting management expectations and an individual's success or otherwise in meeting those expectations

3. Providing a straightforward rationale for appraising and compensating employees fairly

4. Bringing salaries and benefits in line with the employee's length of service

5. Gathering information to be used strictly for salary decisions

Answer

Performance Management

Option 1: This option is correct. Performance appraisals strengthen the bond between participants.

Option 2: This option is correct. Performance management provides a documented record of an employee's work history.

Option 3: This option is correct. Performance management allows employers to assess the value of employees to the organization's objectives and to compensate them accordingly.

Option 4: This option is incorrect. Performance management allows the organization to base compensation on the employee's value to the organization.

Option 5: This option is incorrect. Performance management provides the organization with information to make decisions involving salary, promotions, transfers, career development, and terminations.

Performance standards

Performance standards

The idea of reviewing and appraising performance isn't new. As early as the third century AD, the emperor of China employed a rating system to evaluate his staff. And in the 16th century the Jesuits had a system for formally rating and improving their members. But it wasn't until the late 19th century that the business world adopted "scientific management" – the first widespread formal system of performance appraisal.

Modern performance appraisal involves evaluating each employee's performance to determine that person's value to the organization.

This is done by rating how well the employee meets, or has met, a series of predetermined performance standards. Performance standards are the criteria or benchmarks against which an employee's actual performance is measured.

These standards are often laid out in the employee's performance plan – a written set of expectations agreed to by manager and employee.

Managers must be trained in using an appraisal method that's both efficient and effective for their organization. Most performance appraisals include some form of rating scale that managers can use to indicate different levels of employee achievement in meeting performance standards. Assessments generally consist of ratings for specific job functions, and an average of the total score indicates the employee's overall performance. Rating scales can be alphabetical, numerical, or descriptive, and usually have between three and six levels.

Rating scales benefit employees as well as employers.

Rating scales provide an equitable method of assessing an employee's overall performance and output. They also help determine who is worthy of rewards such as pay increases or promotions.

This approach can also be used to help determine those employees who aren't meeting performance standards, but who have the potential to be trained, coached, and encouraged to achieve higher levels.

Using rating scales

Using rating scales

A common rating tool for performance evaluation is the five-point scale. An example of points in a typical scale would be unsatisfactory, below standard, meets expectations, excellent, and exceptional. The advantage of a five-point scale is that it allows for deviation from a neutral midpoint that represents acceptable performance. But it can be tempting for managers to overuse this midpoint, so it's important to make sure assessors are trained in proper use of their organization's rating methodology.

Each of the points in a rating scale has associated standards that are used as criteria to assess performance.

These standards vary from organization to organization. However, the purpose is always to appraise employees' abilities and success in performing essential job functions.

Performance Management

During a performance assessment the standards are compared to examples of the employee's performance in key job requirements, abilities, and behaviors. This gives the assessor a basis for rating the employee.

Consider Sonical Limited, a manufacturer and distributor of prepared foods. Human resources manager Sandi is working on performance appraisals for a number of employees.

1. Unsatisfactory

Bill works in the Shipping Department. He's failed to show up for work on a number of occasions without notice, and his careless handling of material has resulted in a high rate of damage. Sandi determines that Bill's "performance is well below reasonable standards" and rates it unsatisfactory.

2. Below standard

Dawn is an administrative assistant. She requires a good deal of supervision from her boss to complete work on time. However, she is efficient at taking minutes during executive meetings. Given that Dawn's performance "is stronger is some areas than others," Sandi rates it below standard.

3. Meets expectations

Raoul is a transport driver. He's consistent in meeting schedules and has never had a violation of safety standards. In Sandi's judgment, Raoul's "performance meets expectations" and he "consistently meets standards and targets." So she rates his performance in the third category.

4. Excellent

May is a sales representative. She consistently meets or exceeds her quarterly sales targets, and she's brought in several new customers over the past year. Sandi determines May meets the criteria "superior performance in meeting targets and standards" and "makes notable achievements beyond normal expectations." She rates May's performance as excellent.

5. Exceptional

Priya is a food scientist in the Research and Development Department of the company. She has developed a number of new products that have been very profitable for the company. Priya has turned down several offers to work for other companies, stating her commitment to Sonical. Sandi determines Priya meets the criteria "frequently displays exceptional creativity or initiative" and "demonstrates an outstanding commitment to organizational values."

In a typical assessment, employees will be rated in several categories. Each rating will assess a different aspect or key area of performance.

Although employees usually get an overall rating, this is often cumulative, based on an average of the ratings they achieve in specific areas.

For example an employee could be assessed in the areas of meeting deadlines, procedural knowledge, and communication skills.

Consider Jia. She's a dispatcher for Mathemetric Limited, a logistics company. Jia has recently undergone a performance review where she was rated in a number of different areas of performance. Under the Behavioral category, Jia's manager gave her a four – or excellent – rating for meeting performance standards. Under the Technical Ability category, Jia's performance was rated as

Performance Management

a three – meets expectations. In each case the reviewer noted a brief comment to support the rating.

Jia's ratings are based on how well she met performance standards for each category.

Under the Behavioral category she got an excellent rating because she had consistently met expectations. Her good feedback from the company's drivers was a notable achievement in this area.

Under the Technical Ability category, Jia's manager rated her as meeting expectations. Although Jia is reliably performing in a proficient manner, she will need to complete some training before she can advance to the next level.

Question

Red Rock Construction has just conducted annual performance appraisals.

Match the Red Rock employee to the most appropriate performance appraisal rating. Not all ratings will have a match.

Options:
A. Ginger
B. Kwan
C. Anna
D. James

Targets:
1. Exceptional
2. Excellent
3. Meets expectations
4. Below standard
5. Unsatisfactory

Answer

Ginger's performance is rated as exceptional. Her assessment shows she frequently displays exceptional creativity or initiative.

Kwan's performance is rated as excellent. He shows superior performance in meeting or exceeding his sales targets, and some notable achievements beyond normal expectations.

Anna's performance is rated as meets expectations. Her performance consistently meets standards for her job and she seems well suited to her current role. She reliably performs in a proficient manner.

James's performance is rated as below standard because it is uneven. He meets standards for his carpentry work, but his communication skills are below expectations.

No employees meet the criteria for an unsatisfactory performance rating. None of them are working below reasonable standards or failing to meet essential job requirements. Neither do they demonstrate a lack of commitment to the company or lack of ability to do their job.

Section 2 - Appraising Performance
Section 2 - Appraising Performance

There are two important steps in creating effective performance appraisal meetings. Step one is to plan ahead by preparing yourself and preparing the employee.

Step two is to conduct meetings appropriately. Think of the meeting as having five stages: taking control of the environment and process, discussing the employee's self-evaluation, presenting your own assessment, talking about the employee's future, and bringing the meeting to a close. Follow guidelines for handling each of these stages.

The importance of performance appraisals

The importance of performance appraisals

Performance appraisal meetings are pivotal to the relationship between the manager and the employee. These meetings are key occasions when the two come together to formally discuss the employee's past, present, and future with the organization.

One of the benefits of performance appraisal is that it's an opportunity to build stronger relationships between managers and employees.

Discussing performance in an honest, supportive environment helps employees understand what's expected of them, where they're performing well, and where they need to improve.

It's also a valuable way for employers to understand what impacts employee performance, satisfaction, and retention.

Performance appraisals also encourage constructive employee behaviors. Appraisals strengthen organizational commitment – employees' emotional attachment to, identification with, and positive involvement in the organization. When an organization neglects performance appraisal, it negatively affects workplace morale and ultimately reduces the organization's overall effectiveness.

Poorly implemented performance appraisal meetings can be as detrimental as no appraisal at all. Employees who have been through unproductive appraisal meetings may develop negative feelings, and assume they have no control over the process. Managers who have experienced conflict in a meeting can develop an aversion to giving honest appraisals. Both employer and employee may draw the conclusion that the process is a waste of time.

Negative feelings

Some employees have negative feelings about the performance review process. They see it as an excuse for managers to criticize performance, exert control, or lay the foundation to deny raises or promotions.

No control

Poorly implemented appraisals leave employees feeling they have no control over the process. When the process is perceived as one-sided, employees can give up on performance improvement and become unmotivated and resentful.

Fear of conflict

A poorly designed appraisal program can hinder communication rather than enhance it. Managers can develop a fear of conflict when performance appraisal meetings regularly turn into arguments and disagreements.

Waste of time

When managers dislike and distrust the review process, they consider it a waste of time. Instead of doing appraisals well, they focus on doing them fast. This leaves employees with no clear idea of how well they're doing or how to improve performance.

A balanced, well-structured performance appraisal process is an important workforce development strategy. When appraisal meetings are planned and conducted appropriately, the process can be rewarding and constructive for both employees and managers.

Preparing for the meeting

Preparing for the meeting

There are two steps for making a performance appraisal meeting more effective. Step one is to plan ahead. Step two is to conduct the meeting appropriately. Following the guidelines for each of these steps will help you to create appraisals that are positive and productive for both you and your employees.

Step one of making a performance appraisal meeting more effective is to plan ahead. This involves preparing yourself to conduct the meeting and preparing the employee to participate in the meeting.

To plan ahead for a performance appraisal meeting, you'll have to gather information and data to establish the employee's level of competence.

You'll need evidence to rate the employee's strengths and weaknesses, and to plan strategies to improve performance.

You'll also need to be prepared to present specific examples of the employee's performance to back up your assessments.

So where's the information you need to prepare yourself? It can be found by gathering helpful documentation, and by soliciting information from other people.

There are a number of sources of documentation, including written feedback, notes from training sessions, and records of disciplinary action.

Observation is also a key element in assessing performance. Peers, colleagues, and other managers can be a rich source of information. Coworkers in particular can provide valuable feedback on performance, particularly when it involves teamwork.

You may have noted that because many performance ratings depend on the assessor's judgment, these ratings may be influenced by bias. Types of bias include personal bias, the halo effect, central tendency, recency, and leniency.

Personal bias

Personal bias occurs when an assessor's personal feelings toward an employee influence the ratings. This may be because of a positive personal relationship, such as friendship. Or it could be because of empathy – the tendency to rate people who are like you more favorably. Negative relationships or prejudice can also bias an assessor's rating.

Halo effect

The halo effect occurs when an employee's good performance in one area is carried over into the assessor's evaluation of other areas, resulting in a higher rating than is deserved. For example, a company's top salesperson may be rated highly in job performance and in relationship skills, even if he's difficult to get along with at work.

Central tendency
Central tendency results when an assessor places most performance ratings in the middle of the scale. For example, an assessor may fear making a mistake and so "play it safe" by not discriminating between the employee's strong and weak points.

Recency
Recency bias happens when recently achieved results are weighted more heavily than those achieved earlier in the rating period. For example, a poor performer who improves may be rated higher overall than a good performer who declines.

Leniency
Leniency occurs when an assessor is reluctant to give low ratings and rates employees as average or above average in all areas. Leniency can be triggered by sympathy for the employee, by a desire to be liked, or by an attempt to avoid conflict.

Preparing yourself for conducting a performance appraisal meeting is an important part of planning ahead. But it's just as important to prepare the employee for the meeting. Appraisals that are supported by regular communication throughout the year prepare employees for what's to be discussed during the performance appraisal meeting.

Your appraisal should be a summary of the regular feedback your employee has received throughout the year.

Employees shouldn't be surprised by anything that comes up at their meeting. Neither should they hear about a performance issue for the first time during their appraisal.

In fact, the stronger the mutual understanding between you and your employees, the more productive the meetings are likely to be.

Make sure to plan the meeting in advance, and elicit the support of your employee. At least one week before the meeting, contact the employee to arrange a time and place. Then send the person a written confirmation of the details. Include a self-evaluation form and ask the employee to complete and send it back to you a few days before the meeting.

Question

Zena is a project manager who's planning a performance appraisal for her assistant Aaron.

What are strategies she should use to plan ahead appropriately for Aaron's appraisal?

Options:

1. Talk to the other members of her team about Aaron's teamwork and communication skills

2. Check with the Human Resources Department to access Aaron's recent training records

3. Make sure her personal assessment of Aaron is objective

4. Use the feedback she's given Aaron throughout the year as the basis of her assessment

5. Contact Aaron a week prior to the appraisal to arrange a time and place to meet

6. Wait until the meeting to tell Aaron about any performance problems

Performance Management

7. Don't give Aaron any rating lower than average

Answer

Option 1: This option is correct. Soliciting information from others will give Zena valuable insight into Aaron's performance.

Option 2: This option is correct. Gathering helpful documentation such as training records can help Zena determine where Aaron is excelling and where he needs to improve.

Option 3: This option is correct. Striving to avoid bias is important to producing a fair and accurate assessment.

Option 4: This option is correct. Zena's appraisal will be more productive if she avoids surprising Aaron with unexpected information.

Option 5: This option is correct. Arranging details with Aaron in advance of the meeting is an important part of careful preparation.

Option 6: This option is incorrect. No surprises should be sprung on Aaron during the meeting.

Option 7: This option is incorrect. Leniency is a form of bias.

Conducting the appraisal meeting

Conducting the appraisal meeting

Step two of making a performance appraisal meeting more effective is to conduct the meeting appropriately. This can be done by following a structured five-stage approach. First, take control. Second, discuss the employee's self-evaluation. Third, present your own assessment. Fourth, talk about the employee's future, and fifth, conclude the meeting.

1. Take control

Stage one is to take control of the environment and assessment process. Welcome the employee to the meeting and put the person at ease. State the purpose of the meeting and explain what the format will be.

2. Discuss self-evaluation

Stage two is to discuss the employee's self-evaluation. These ratings should reflect the same areas and criteria you used in your assessment.

3. Present your assessment

Stage three involves presenting your assessment of the employee's performance. This is where you cover the employee's strengths and weaknesses, and explain how the ratings were reached.

4. Talk about future

Stage four is where you and the employee talk about the future. Here you'd help the employee set performance goals for the coming year, and determine training needs to help improve job skills and opportunities for advancement.

5. Conclude meeting

Stage five is to conclude the meeting by summarizing what's been agreed to and having the employee sign the assessment.

Laurel is the senior manager at a luxury hotel. She's conducting a performance review with Marco, the hotel's reservations manager.

Consider how Laurel conducts the first two stages in the performance appraisal process.

Laurel: Thanks for meeting with me, Marco. I know it's a busy time of the year for you.

Laurel is pleasant.

Marco: We had quite a rush this morning. A big tour group checked in and needed some extra rooms.

Marco is friendly.

Laurel: Well, let me outline things for you. First we'll discuss your self-evaluation. Next I'll present my assessment. And then we'll talk about our goals for the future. Sound OK?

Laurel is asking.

Marco: Fine.

Marco is agreeable.

Laurel: I see you rated yourself a three out of five for communication skills. Is that right?

Laurel is looking at the evaluation.

Marco: Yes.

Marco is agreeable.

Laurel: OK then. Shall we move on?

Laurel is asking.

Marco: Sure.

Marco is agreeable.

Question

Which stage of Marco's appraisal did Laurel conduct appropriately?

Options:

1. Stage one - take control
2. Stage two - discuss self-evaluation

Answer

Option 1: This is the correct option. Laurel started off Marco's assessment meeting well. In stage one she took control of the environment and process. She put Marco at ease and clearly stated the purpose and format of the meeting.

Option 2: This option is incorrect. Laurel didn't do so well in stage two of the appraisal – discussing Marco's self-evaluation. She didn't use some basic communication techniques that would have encouraged Marco to open up and participate in the discussion.

Using communication techniques

Using communication techniques

It's important to get employees to talk about their performance during their self-evaluation. This can be achieved by using communication techniques such as active listening and open-ended questions. Employees are more likely to participate when they know that you're listening and they sense you're interested in what they have to say.

Active listening is a way of listening and responding to another person that encourages open communication. When you're actively listening to someone, you should provide verbal feedback to indicate you're interested.

Don't interrupt. Encourage the speaker to continue by using short phrases and interjections to show you're listening: "Yes, I understand" or "Go on." If the conversation warrants, you could consider more direct prompts like: "What are your feelings about that?" or "How did you react?"

One active listening technique is to paraphrase what the speaker has said. This demonstrates you're paying attention. You might say "So what you're saying is you like working on a team" or "You're saying you've helped boost sales for your department."

Questions are also an important part of encouraging conversation. Open-ended questions are phrased to elicit full, meaningful answers. They encourage employees to become involved in a dialogue, rather than just replying with disconnected "yes" or "no" answers.

Open-ended questions implicitly offer an invitation to employees to consider, evaluate, interpret, and define the issues under discussion.

Open-ended questions typically begin with words such as "How" or "What" or phrases such as "Tell me about..." Sometimes they're phrased as a statement that implicitly asks for a response. For example, you might say "Let's explore how that works" or "Tell me about your idea."

Question

Match each statement or question to the principle it demonstrates.

Options:

A. "I'm glad to be able to meet with you today."

B. "We're here to discuss your performance appraisal."

C. "What was your rationale for rating your productivity as excellent?"

D. "I understand. Go on."

Targets:

1. Put the employee at ease
2. State the purpose and format of the assessment

3. Use open-ended questions
4. Use active listening techniques

Answer

In stage one you put employees at ease by welcoming them and showing interest.

In stage one you explain the purpose and format of the process to help the employee understand the review process.

In stage two, using open-ended questions will elicit full, meaningful answers and encourage the employee to become involved in the conversation.

In stage two, active listening involves using short phrases and interjections to show you're interested.

Presenting the assessment

Presenting the assessment

Laurel's performance review with her employee Marco is in progress. Follow along as she conducts the third stage in the performance appraisal process – presenting her assessment.

Laurel: So that covers your self-assessment. Let's go through my assessment of your performance.

Laurel is pleasant.

Marco: I'm ready.

Marco is friendly.

Laurel: For "Adaptability" you rated yourself three, but I gave you four. I think you really work well under pressure. Look at how you handled the tour group this morning.

Marco: I do try to stay calm.

Marco is pleased.

Laurel: Now under "Interpersonal Skills", you gave yourself four, but I had three. You're great on the front-desk team, but you can be impatient with new staff.

Marco: Well, it's frustrating when they don't catch on quickly...

Marco is begrudgingly agreeing.

Laurel: That's not their fault, it's yours. You can be a little arrogant. So what do you think we could do to remedy this?

Laurel is reprimanding.

Marco: Extra training for new staff maybe? I just don't have time to show them how to do things over and over.

Marco is cooperative but not happy.

Laurel: Come to me if they need more training and I'll arrange it. And your new performance goal will be to remain patient with the new staff.

Laurel is smiling.

Laurel was successful in some areas of stage three - presenting her assessment. She was positive about Marco's strengths and she was candid and specific about his weakness.

However, Laurel would have been better to focus on Marco's behavior, rather than point out personal traits and assign blame for issues.

Laurel did work with Marco to resolve the issue and to set a new performance goal for him. However she should have asked him for his reaction to her assessment.

Stage three is probably the most important part of the performance appraisal for the assessor. Make sure to present your assessment in a positive manner.

Tell the employee what was done well, and deliver any criticism constructively. Be candid and specific in your statements, and ensure your feedback is clear, objective, and encouraging.

Highlight the employees's strengths, but don't ignore issues that need attention. For example you might say, "Your teamwork skills are excellent, but we need to set some goals to enhance your personal initiative in the future."

When presenting your assessments, it's critical to focus on specific behaviors, not personality traits.

Don't blame the employee for any low ratings. Instead, use examples of behavior to back up your assessment.

For example, a statement such as "You seem incapable of getting your monthly reports in on time" is far less powerful than saying "Ten out of your twelve monthly reports were late this year."

Successful performance often involves interaction among employees who work as a team. Your appraisals should cover teamwork skills such as collaborative ability and reliability.

Remember too that the assessment is a cooperative exercise. Ask for the employee's reaction to each of your assessments. Letting employees communicate their opinions will reinforce the importance of their participation.

Statements such as "Tell me how you feel about that," or "Do you feel this is fair?" can open up the conversation. This will allow you to make suggestions for improvement, and help you to problem-solve together with the employee.

Question

Andrew is a manager at a bank. He's presenting an assessment to an employee during an appraisal meeting.

Performance Management

Match the statements or questions to principles that he's applying.

Options:

A. "Your productivity increased this year."

B. "We need to discuss improving your communication skills."

C. "You had a 20% increase in customer complaints this year."

D. "Your coworkers report you're very dependable for meeting deadlines."

E. "How do you feel about that rating?"

Targets:

1. Be positive
2. Don't ignore issues that need attention
3. Focus on behaviors
4. Cover teamwork
5. Ask for employee's reaction

Answer

Being positive includes telling employees what they did right.

It's important to be candid and specific when discussing behaviors that need attention.

You shouldn't blame the employee, but instead present specific examples of behaviors to back up your assessments.

Assessments should cover teamwork as well as individual performance.

Asking for an employee's reaction will reinforce the importance of participation.

Concluding the appraisal meeting

Concluding the appraisal meeting

Stage four of conducting a performance appraisal is to talk about the future. Let the employee take the lead here, and offer your support to set performance and training goals for the coming year. Make sure each goal is SMART – specific, measurable, achievable, relevant, and timely.

Specific

Specific goals state exactly what's to be accomplished.

Measurable

Measurable goals state the standard against which success will be assessed.

Achievable

Achievable goals include conditions under which the goal can realistically be achieved.

Relevant

Performance Management

Relevant goals are within areas of authority or control of the employee.

Timely

Timely goals include a time reference, such as a specific deadline.

A SMART performance goal might read "Submit budget reports by the last working day of each month" or "Address any discrepancies in the sales reports within five days of receiving the document."

A SMART training goal could be "Take the project management training workshop starting July 5." Stage five of conducting a performance appraisal is to conclude the meeting.

First, summarize the discussion you just had – the positive behaviors and results you'd like to continue, the areas that need improvement, and the next period's performance and developmental goals. Have the employee sign the written assessment and schedule any interim follow-up if needed.

Finally, make sure to end the assessment on a positive note. Here you could say "I think our time has been well spent. I'm confident that you'll achieve the goals we've outlined. Remember that I'm always here to help you if you want to discuss this further."

Question

Match each stage of conducting an effective performance appraisal meeting with a principle or action required at that stage.

Options:

A. 1. Take control
B. 2. Discuss self-evaluation
C. 3. Present your assessment

D. 4. Talk about the future

E. 5. Conclude the meeting

Targets:

1. State the purpose and format of the assessment meeting.

2. Use open-ended questions and active listening techniques.

3. Focus on behaviors, not personality traits. Ask for the employee's reaction to the appraisal.

4. Let the employee lead the discussion, and work together to set performance and training goals.

5. Summarize what's been discussed and have the employee sign the assessment.

Answer

You need to be clear about the purpose and format of the appraisal meeting at the start.

It's important to use open-ended questions and active listening techniques to encourage participation during stage two of the meeting.

Focusing on specific behaviors and asking for the employee's reaction to the assessment is part of stage three.

Working with the employee to set goals for improved future performance is part of stage four.

Stage five involves summarizing the meeting and asking the employee to sign the assessment. This demonstrates a shared understanding of the events of the meeting.

Section 3 - Conducting a Performance Appraisal Meeting

Section 3 - Conducting a Performance Appraisal Meeting

Good interpersonal communication is particularly important during stages two and three of the performance appraisal meeting. These are the stages when you discuss the employee's self-evaluation and present your assessment. During an employee's self-evaluation, you should use open-ended questions to encourage participation. Also, use active listening techniques such as paraphrasing to show you're interested.

When you present your assessment, be positive and highlight employees' strengths. But make sure not to avoid discussing problem behaviors. Make suggestions for improvement, and problem-solve with the employee.

Cover both teamwork and individual contributions in the appraisal, and make sure to ask for the employee's reaction before you conclude the meeting.

Stages of performance appraisal meetings

Stages of performance appraisal meetings

The five-stage process for conducting an effective performance appraisal meeting lets you balance practical feedback and emotional support. This gives employees direction and encouragement to improve job performance. Stage one is taking control of the environment and the process. Stage two is discussing the employee's self-evaluation. Stage three is presenting your own assessment. Stage four is talking about the employee's future, and stage five is concluding the meeting.

1. Take control

In stage one you take control of the environment and process by putting the employee at ease and stating the purpose and format of the assessment.

2. Discuss self-evaluation

Stage two involves discussing the employee's self-evaluation and encouraging participation by using open-ended questions and active listening techniques.

3. Present your assessment

Stage three is when you present your assessment. Here you cover the employee's individual and team-related behavior, and then ask for the employee's reaction to your assessment. Make sure to be positive, candid, and specific.

4. Talk about future

Stage four involves discussing the employee's future, and setting performance and training goals.

5. Conclude meeting

The final stage is when you bring the meeting to a close. Here you summarize the meeting, have the employee sign the assessment, and schedule follow-up if necessary. Be sure to end the meeting on a positive note.

Good communication builds productive relationships, and performance appraisal meetings can be an excellent opportunity to create an effective dialogue with your employees.

Much of the communication that happens during a performance appraisal takes place during stage two – discussing the employee's self-evaluation – and stage three – presenting your assessment.

In this topic you'll have the chance to practice conducting stages two and three of a performance appraisal meeting.

Section 4 - Rewarding Performance

Formal reward programs are a way of determining a fair and equitable basis for rewarding and compensating employees. Many organizations have formal reward programs that are directly linked to performance appraisal. These programs clearly connect performance and reward, provide appropriate rewards, ensure fairness, and reward both group and individual contributions.

One of the most common compensation methods is fixed percentage pay increases. Pay increases are based on the employee's overall performance ratings and awarded by a series of predetermined fixed percentages.

The importance of rewarding employees

The importance of rewarding employees

Employers appraise performance for a number of reasons. Performance appraisals are often used to support Human Resources decisions regarding such things as training needs, succession planning, promotions, transfers, and terminations. But arguably the most important function of performance appraisal is to determine a fair and equitable basis for rewarding and compensating employees.

Rewards are the most effective way of recognizing and encouraging good performance from both individuals and groups. But not all types of rewards motivate everyone equally. The key to performance management is identifying the right balance of extrinsic and intrinsic motivators. If you neglect either type, it can have a detrimental effect – employees will feel you don't appreciate them, or that you don't value the work they do.

Both extrinsic and intrinsic rewards are needed to satisfy and motivate employees.

Intrinsic

Intrinsic motivators are emotional rewards such as respect, recognition, interest, enjoyment, passion, creative challenge, and fulfillment. These rewards come from carrying out work activity rather than from compensation for completing the activity.

For example, a graphic artist might be motivated by the creative challenge of his work, and turn down a higher paying administrative job.

Extrinsic

Extrinsic motivators are material rewards such as bonuses, salary increases, time off, stock options, or a company car.

For example, a salesperson on commission may be motivated by an extrinsic reward – money. She will feel undervalued with just a pat on the back.

Recognition and reward should be an ongoing, natural part of an employee's day-to-day work experience.

This could be as simple as saying "thanks" for a job well done, or something more formal like a bonus, or extra time off.

Acknowledging employees affirms they're doing a good job. Employees will quickly become disengaged if they feel discounted, excluded, or ignored.

Question

Match the reward to its appropriate type.

Options:

A. Company car
B. Respect
C. Praise

D. Salary
Targets:
1. Extrinsic
2. Intrinsic
Answer

Extrinsic rewards satisfy material needs and can be valued in terms of monetary worth. These include salary, bonuses, and "perks" such as a company car.

Intrinsic rewards satisfy emotional needs. These include praise, freedom, respect, and enjoyment.

Efficient rewards practices

Efficient rewards practices

Many organizations tie compensation only to tangible rewards such as cash. They give little consideration to the intangible value of rewards such as prestige, work culture, or training and development opportunities. But an effective rewards program encompasses these types of rewards as well as monetary compensation.

You'd be right if you noted that in the long term, job satisfaction is influenced more strongly by intrinsic rewards.

Although extrinsic rewards remain significant for short-term motivation, employees are more satisfied with their work when also provided with recognition, enjoyment, and opportunities for personal growth.

Recognition and rewards programs are a way of formalizing the value exchange between an organization and its employees. Many organizations have formal rewards programs that are directly linked to performance appraisals. The most effective and efficient rewards programs clearly connect performance and reward, provide appropriate rewards, ensure fairness, and reward both group and individual contributions.

In an effective rewards program there is a clear connection between performance and reward. Rewards are tied to employees' performance assessment ratings, as well as to their specific and significant achievements.

An organization's rewards system deals with its salary and benefits structure, but may also include informal rewards and recognitions. Because people are motivated by different things, it's important that the system provide employees with appropriate rewards.

For example, some people may be motivated by money, while others may respond better to being given more creative freedom.

Good rewards programs should also be fair and equitable. Rewards and performance criteria should be announced in advance, and made accessible to everyone.

The criteria must be understandable and achievable so employees will be motivated, rather than frustrated by trying to meet the standards set.

In addition, good programs will reward both group and individual contributions. The contribution individuals make to the success of their department, project team, or other business unit will be recognized and rewarded.

Effective rewards programs also recognize that employees assess the value of both intrinsic and extrinsic rewards in relation to how many others at work also enjoy those rewards.

People tend to be more highly motivated by specific rewards – those that are well defined and related to their individual wants and needs. These include salary, perks, recognition, prestige, and promotion. General rewards are more widely applied to larger groups or categories of employees. This would include overall working conditions.

But although general rewards are not a significant motivational force, the lack of general rewards can severely demotivate employees. For example employees rarely think about enjoying a comfortable or safe environment, but will react negatively if they feel uncomfortable or unsafe at work.

Earth Farm Herbs is an agricultural corporation with a well-established rewards system.

Clearly connects performance and reward

The company has a well-organized and transparent performance appraisal program that is aligned with its compensation and rewards program, retention strategy, and succession plans. This information is communicated to all employees.

Provides appropriate rewards

The company has a balanced rewards program that provides both intrinsic and extrinsic rewards. The company provides regular bonuses for individuals and teams that meet performance targets. It also provides high achievers with career counseling and promotions if they desire.

Ensures fairness

The company adheres to a formal structure for compensation, and awards bonuses to employees for high performance. Managers are open and transparent about the implementation of processes that allocate resources, and the company has a structure in place to resolve disputes.

Rewards group and individual contribution

Within the rewards system, the company breaks down its corporate goals into specific performance objectives for each division, department, team, and individual employees. Rewards are distributed on the basis of profit-sharing.

Question

Sonical Logistics has an established rewards system.

What are examples of the company applying the principles of efficient rewards practices?

Options:

1. The company has a well-organized and transparent performance appraisal program

2. The company's rewards include bonuses, time-off, awards, and public acknowledgment of achievements

3. The implementation of the program is open and transparent, and is conducted to approved standards

4. Within the program, rewards are tied to performance goals defined by division, department, team, and individual

5. The organization's reward system deals strictly with monetary compensation

6. Employees' compensation is based on a base salary with a bonus based on length of service

Answer

Option 1: This option is correct. The company's appraisal program connects employees' performance and rewards.

Option 2: This option is correct. The company provides appropriate rewards by offering a balance of intrinsic and extrinsic rewards.

Option 3: This option is correct. Ensuring fairness is an important principle of efficient rewards practices.

Option 4: This option is correct. The company rewards both group and individual contributions.

Option 5: This option is incorrect. An efficient rewards system balances both intrinsic and extrinsic rewards.

Option 6: This option is incorrect. An efficient rewards system ties performance to reward.

Benefits of an efficient rewards system

Benefits of an efficient rewards system

There are many advantages to an organization maintaining an effective rewards system. Rewards engage and motivate employees. This ultimately increases both individual and team productivity. Rewards can also help with the recruitment and retention of valuable employees, attracting professionals who thrive in performance-based environments. A performance-based rewards system also increases employees' sense of commitment and stimulates their interest in the organization's financial performance.

Unito Foods is a manufacturer of prepared frozen food. The company depends on a skilled workforce to maintain high-quality standards and generate innovative new products. The company offers a safe and comfortable workplace. It has flexible work schedules, accessible parking, and other general rewards.

Recently Unito Foods expanded its rewards system to include a plan linking specific rewards to corporate performance. It now awards cash bonuses based on individual and team performance.

Bonus amounts are based on a formula determined by the company's annual cost savings and increase in sales. The company has also tied its succession planning program to employee performance, encouraging high performers to stay with the company.

Unito's program balances extrinsic and intrinsic rewards, and offers specific rewards tied to performance. Since its inception, the program has contributed to increased sales, lower production costs, and an improved employee retention rate.

Question

What are the benefits of an efficient rewards system?

Options:

1. It helps attract and retain high-performing employees

2. It encourages employees' interest in the organization's financial performance

3. It encourages employees to work as a team

4. It instills a sense of ownership in the organization's success

5. Productivity will be encouraged

6. The organization will increase its profits

7. Employees will make more money than with a flat salary

Answer

Option 1: This option is correct. Results-driven professionals thrive in a performance-based environment.

Option 2: This option is correct. Employees will be more interested in an organization's financial performance if rewards are tied to it.

Option 3: This option is correct. A rewards program tied to organizational performance encourages employees to work together.

Option 4: This option is correct. Employees who are rewarded fairly have a greater commitment to their organization.

Option 5: This option is correct. A fair and efficient rewards system shows employees the connection between productivity and rewards.

Option 6: This option is incorrect. A rewards system can't be structured to guarantee a profit, but it will encourage employees' interest in the organizations's financial health.

Option 7: This option is incorrect. Not all employees will reap rewards, but more valuable employees will benefit from a performance-driven rewards system.

Linking pay rewards to performance

Linking pay rewards to performance

Would you go to work every day if you never got paid? Probably not.

Employees are motivated by many different types of rewards, but pay represents the foundation of the employment relationship.

In many organizations, there's a system in place for aligning pay to performance. This is known as performance pay, or simply merit pay.

There are a number of ways to convert assessments of people's performance into decisions about remuneration and reward. One of the most common approaches is using fixed percentage pay increases.

In this approach, the employee's annual pay is increased by previously determined fixed percentages. These increases are tied to the performance category standards set forth in the company's performance appraisal program.

Pay increases are based on the employee's overall performance ratings and awarded by a series of fixed percentages. The percentages and methods of calculation will vary from company to company.

Consider Whitney, a sales associate at Gleeson Associates, a financial services company. The company uses fixed percentage pay increases based on a five-point performance rating scale. The scale gives one point for unsatisfactory, two points for below standard, three points for meets expectations, four points for excellent, and five points for exceptional. At Whitney's annual performance appraisal she's assessed in six different performance categories. Her scores are added and averaged to an overall score of four or "Excellent."

Gleeson Associates has a fixed percentage attached to each category in the performance appraisal scale. This is used to determine an employee's annual pay raise. Since Whitney has an overall performance rating of excellent, this corresponds to a 3.5% increase in her annual salary.

Question

Phlogistix Consulting uses a performance-based pay scale to compensate employees. Match the employee to the appropriate pay raise. Not all pay raises will have a match.

Options:
A. Bill
B. Gordon
C. Sita

Targets:
1. 2% raise 2. 1% raise 3. 3.5% raise 4. 0% raise

Answer

Bill's overall rating is a three. This entitles him to a 2% pay raise.

Gordon's overall rating is a two. This entitles him to a 1% pay raise.

Sita's overall rating is a four. This entitles her to a 3.5% pay raise.

No employee scored a one, which equals a 0% pay raise.

REFERENCES

References
Performance Management - 2000, Charles M. Cadwell, Citation
Performance Management: Key Strategies and Practical Guidelines, 3rd Edition - 2006, Michael Armstrong, Citation
Armstrong's Essential Human Resource Management Practice: A Guide to People Management - 2010, Michael Armstrong, Kogan Page
Performance Dashboards: Measuring, Monitoring, and Managing Your Business - 2011, Wayne Eckerson, John Wiley & Sons
Managing Your Career For Dummies - 2000, Max Messmer, John Wiley & Sons
Organizational Behavior, 11th Edition - 2010, John R. Schermerhorn, Jr., James G. Hunt, Richard N. Osborn and Mary Uhl-Bien, John Wiley & Sons
Armstrong's Handbook of Reward Management Practice: Improving Performance

Through Reward, 3rd Edition - 2010, Michael Armstrong, Kogan Page

Performance Planning and Review: Making Employee Appraisals Work, 2nd Edition - 2003, Richard Rudman, Allen & Unwin

Quest for Balance: The Human Element in Performance Management Systems - 2002, Andre A. De Waal, John Wiley & Sons

www.ingramcontent.com/pod-product-compliance
Lightning Source LLC
Chambersburg PA
CBHW020912180526
45163CB00007B/2705